Favorite Recipes of J

The Oke Family Cookbook

COLLECTED BY

DEBORAH OKE & BARBARA OKE

BETHANY HOUSE PUBLISHERS

MINNEAPOLIS, MINNESOTA 55438
A Division of Bethany Fellowship, Inc.

Published by Bethany House Publishers
A Ministry of Bethany Fellowship, Inc.
11300 Hampshire Avenue South
Minneapolis, Minnesota 55438

Printed in the United States of America

CONTENTS

INTRODUCTION

I hadn't realized how revealing it would be to dig through recipe files, but I discovered that the very fabric of family is woven throughout the hastily scribbled memos and carefully penned cards.

New brides, still with a blush to their silky cheeks, copiously borrowed from mother, grandmothers, aunts, and sisters-in-law recipes that had been tried and proven by many young brides before them. The files grew, filled handwritten scribblers, and were passed on from generation to generation.

In searching through the recipes with my two daughters-in-law I was amazed at how often a favorite recipe would turn up. Everyone in the family seemed to have the recipe for Margaret's Cake even though no one seemed to know who Margaret was.

Recipes—family—sharing—they all seem tied together. Not only are traditions passed on, but a special bonding takes place between one generation of cooks and another—one age of homemakers and another—a legacy of love to help the younger set establish a home.

I am thankful to have recipes used by my mother, my grandmothers, and even my great-grandmother. I am glad that I can pass the recipes on to my daughters—and they in turn to their daughters.

Much has changed since the years when Great-grandmother baked her homemade bread, but the need for family has not changed. God designed the family as part of His great plan. He knew how much we would need each other. Today we need to take advantage of every possible way to foster the sense of family, build on our traditions, and pass on a legacy of love. One simple way to strengthen the family bond is to pass on family recipes.

Grandmother not only had to concern herself with what to cook for dinner; she also had to have recipes for other household needs. The following two recipes give a glimpse into her weekly tasks. These "how-tos" were important for the new bride.

HARD SOAP
GRANDMA VIOLET RUGGLES

5 gallons of soft water	one package good soap flakes
2 cans lye	10 pounds fat
3 tablespoons resin	$1^1/_2$ cups gasoline
$^1/_2$ pound borax	

Put water in tub on stove. Add lye and borax and stir well.

When boiling add resin (powdered fine). Stir until melted. Then add the hot, strained fat and finally soap flakes. Boil for 2$^1/_2$ hours. Set aside to cool and add gasoline. Pour into pans. When cold, cut into bars.

I'm glad I don't have to make this recipe for my weekly laundry. It sounds a bit "explosive."

Here's another of Grandma's recipes.

TO REMOVE BLACK LETTERING FROM SUGAR AND FLOUR SACKS

Put sacking in a large pan half filled with water, adding a pint of kerosene and one cup or more of soap. Heat and stir during one day and overnight. Then rinse and put into clean cool water containing bleach solution. When bags are snowy white, remove them, wash in soapsuds, rinse and dry. They look like linen when pressed and dry.

Sugar and flour sacks provided much of the material for household items. I still like teatowels made from the material. Once they are broken in they are wonderfully absorbent and lint-free. But it is difficult to find the material today. And then they must be properly bleached and hemmed. It is much easier to run to the local K-Mart and buy ready-made towels.

We got a real chuckle out of the following recipe found in my Aunt Laurine's cookbook. I have no idea who Lorena Sibley is or was. Nor do I know if the recipe is real or was someone's idea of a joke. All I know is that I have never been served groundhog at a family dinner.

LORENA SIBLEY'S GROUNDHOG

8 to 10 pound groundhog, cleaned and dressed
salted water
teaspoon salt
1 whole onion

flour seasoned with salt and pepper
1 cup butter
4 tablespoons oil

Cut legs and back into serving size pieces. Discard rest. Soak meat overnight in salted water. Rinse carefully. Place in a kettle with salt and onions. Cover with cold water; bring to a boil. Turn down the heat and simmer until tender. Drain. Dry with towel. Dredge with seasoned flour and brown in hot oil and butter. Makes 8 to 10 servings.

I think I could serve a crowd of 100 with this and still have plenty left over. I can't imagine anyone pigging out!

GRANDMA RUGGLES

There are no words to adequately describe my Grandmother Ruggles. To me, she was everything that a grandmother is meant to be. Patient, kind, thoughtful, and filled with concern for all—not just her family, but for friend, neighbor, and stranger alike.

Oh, I don't suppose she was a saint. She must have had times when she felt anger, bitterness, maybe even envy—but I don't remember ever seeing it.

John Archibald Ruggles
& Violet Dell (Gray)

I do remember her home-baked breads and cakes presented to neighbors at opportune times, her scurrying about to wait on guests, her gentle words of encouragement, and even her soft words of correction. I also remember her sense of humor. She enjoyed a good joke—especially if it was on herself.

She was a simple woman as far as the world's standard of fashion was concerned. She was neat and tidy and grandmotherly—never fussing to

GENERATIONS OF COOKS

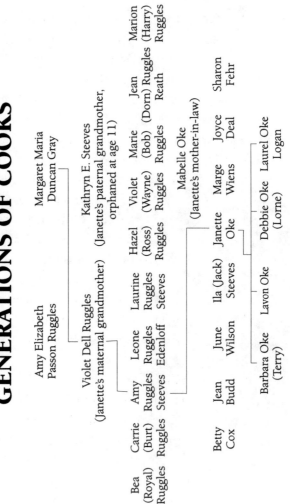

Amy Elizabeth
Passon Ruggles

Margaret Maria
Duncan Gray

Kathryn E. Steeves
(Janette's paternal grandmother,
orphaned at age 11)

Violet Dell Ruggles
(Janette's maternal grandmother)

Bea
(Royal)
Ruggles

Carrie
(Burt)
Ruggles

Amy
Ruggles
Steeves

Leone
Ruggles
Edenloff

Laurine
Ruggles
Steeves

Hazel
(Ross)
Ruggles

Violet
(Wayne)
Ruggles

Marie
(Bob)
Ruggles

Jean
(Dorn) Ruggles
Reath

Marion
(Harry)
Ruggles

Mabelle Oke
(Janette's mother-in-law)

Betty
Cox

Jean
Budd

June
Wilson

Ila (Jack)
Steeves

Janette
Oke

Marge
Wiens

Joyce
Deal

Sharon
Fehr

Barbara Oke
(Terry)

Lavon Oke

Debbie Oke
(Lorne)

Laurel Oke
Logan

make herself appear to be something she was not. So she had a good laugh one day after a visit to the hairdresser. Her eyes sparkled with humor as she relayed the little story.

"After the hairdresser washed my hair she asked me, 'Do you want a rinse?' I thought that a rather silly question, but I said, 'Yes.'"

Then Grandma chuckled as she indicated her head of silver hair. It now was a lovely bluish color.

Grandmother Ruggles raised a family of ten—seven sons and three daughters. And there wasn't a black sheep in the lot. But it was not until she was a grown woman with married children that she really understood that her belief in God must also include a personal acceptance of Christ's atonement on her behalf. It was in those years that her sons and daughters also began to experience a personal relationship to Christ as their Savior. One by one they took that all-important step of faith, and in turn began to raise their children to follow Christ's bidding.

Royal, her firstborn, married Bea Scott.

Burt married Carrie Sanderson.

Amy (my mother), first daughter, married Fred Steeves.

Leone, one of the twins, married Walter Edenloff.

Laurine, the other twin, married Fred's younger brother, Jack Steeves.

Ross wed Hazel Chapman.

Wayne married Hazel's sister Violet.

Bob married Marie Hansen.

Dorn married Jean Tindall, and Jean, after losing Dorn to a heart attack, later married Jim Reath.

Harry, the baby of the family, married Marion Johnson.

AMY STEEVES

I have often heard others say, "Amy can make a tasty meal out of nothing." I'm not sure that was true—but it was true that she often cooked with a rather lean cupboard and little time to fuss when unexpected guests showed up. But it never seemed to unnerve her. She fixed what she had and offered it with sincere hospitality, and folks always seemed to feel honored to sit at her table.

It reminds me of a saying that I have often repeated to myself in an effort to really understand and believe the words: "Give what you have. To some it may be better than you dare to think" (Henry Wadsworth Longfellow).

I think Mom really believed that. She offered what she had freely and graciously, and people accepted her offering with deep appreciation. No one was turned from her door—it would not have mattered if the person were a tramp or a king. I confess that I do not remember kings coming around very frequently, but I do remember some tramps. And they were fed both physical and spiritual food before being sent on their way.

I was blessed with sisters. Lots of sisters. Older sisters and younger sisters. Sisters who left home before I started off to school, and a baby sister whom I hardly knew as a child. There was a twenty-year span between the oldest and the youngest of us, and because we needed to go off to school for our education past the eighth or ninth grade, we moved in and out of home and off to relatives for boarding beginning at an early age.

Amazingly, the first time we were all together for an event was for Mom's seventieth birthday. Up until that time one or another of us was always missing.

There are seven of us girls and I am right in the middle. Each sister has her own special place in my heart—her own special set of memories that I treasure. In order—Betty, Jean, June, my brother Jack, me, Margie, Joyce, and then Sharon. Sharon was

Grandma Amy Steeves & girls
L-R: Janette, Jean, Betty, Ila (Jack's wife), Joyce, Margie
Seated: Grandma & Sharon
Missing: June

born an auntie to one nephew, Betty's oldest son, and a second nephew, born to Jean, soon joined the family to be Sharon's playmate and then soul-mate through the years.

We shared many things through our years of growing up. One of our greatest joys and pleasures is that we are still sharing.

GRANDMOTHER STEEVES

I hardly knew my Grandmother Steeves. In fact, my memories of her embrace only one occasion—when she came to care for the

family while my mother went to her parents' home to give birth to Joyce, second youngest in our family.

Grandmother Steeves was a pioneer woman—though not by choice, I think. Orphaned at the age of eleven, she went to live with an older sister and her family. It was a well-off family in New Brunswick, and Grandmother was given all of the amenities available at the time, including a good education.

Kathryn Estelle Steeves

She became a teacher, married Grandfather, and lived in a lovely big home in the rolling countryside until the death of their baby girl. Then Grandfather decided to move West. Grandmother left her beautiful, big three-story home to live in a small, crowded, prairie dwelling where the wind blew without ceasing, sweeping dust into every corner and crack.

Grandmother kept her dignity and trained her sons in gentlemanly arts—but it must have been terribly difficult for her. She died of cancer when I was still young. I feel I owe her much—for she gave to me a most wonderful daddy.

MABELLE OKE

My mother-in-law, Mabelle Oke, cooks like she does everything else—very well. When our kids were small it was always a big treat for them to go to Grandmother's house for dinner—though I must admit that they were far more impressed with her great desserts than with her creamed cauliflower or steamed broccoli.

Our family always looked

Grandmother Mabelle Oke and Ashley

forward to Christmas with grandparents. Uncle Vern Hannah often prepared the morning breakfast—hash browns, ham, and scrambled eggs. Then at dinner Grandpa carved the turkey and Grandmother served it with her special whipped potatoes, stuffing, and gravy. Sweet potatoes were always one of the vegetables, and the meal always included a tasty salad and often some of her special corn fritters. For dessert we might have some of her steamed pudding with sauce. If one of us was too full, we just waited and enjoyed it later.

Grandmother's Christmas cookies were always special, and we adult "cooks" appreciated them as much if not more than the children because we knew how much time they took to prepare.

It was traditional at Grandmother's house to have Christmas Crackers. Each of them had a funny little hat inside that was to be worn for the meal, a joke or riddle, and a little trinket. After "pulling" his or her cracker, each family member shared with others the joke and then played with the trinket while waiting to be served.

All of the little cousins—and there were eight in all—could hardly wait for another Christmas at Grandmother's house.

All of the above have contributed to my life in many ways. One of the ways has been evident in my recipe files. Favorite recipes have been generously shared. May you enjoy them too.

May you also enjoy the short family stories that I have interspersed throughout the book.

—Janette Oke

1
...
Appetizers

AMY'S CRACKER DIP

Janette Oke

■ ■ ■ ■ ■ ■ ■ ■ ■ ■ ■ ■

INGREDIENTS

1 8-ounce package cream
  cheese
$1/2$ cup sour cream
$1/2$ cup Miracle Whip
1 jar cocktail sauce

1 can shrimp
2 cups grated cheddar cheese
1 small pepper (diced)
3 green onions (diced)
2 tomatoes (diced)

PREPARATION

Blend cream cheese, sour cream, and Miracle Whip; spread on pie plate. Spread in layers the cocktail sauce, shrimp, cheese, pepper, onions, and tomatoes. Refrigerate and let set 2 hours.

  Variation: Same as above except delete sour cream and use 1 cup Miracle Whip, omit shrimp, or use less cheddar.

■ ■ ■ ■ ■ ■ ■ ■ ■ ■ ■ ■

**Eating slowly helps to keep one slim:
in other words, haste makes waist.**

A. H. Hallock

FRUIT DIP

Aunt Joyce Deal

INGREDIENTS

1/4 cup mayonnaise
2 teaspoons honey
1/2 teaspoon finely grated
  orange rind

2 teaspoons orange juice
1/2 cup whipping cream
  (whipped)

PREPARATION

Blend all ingredients. Use as dip with fresh fruits.

NACHO BEAN PLATTER

Barbara Oke

INGREDIENTS

1 can deep brown beans
1 tablespoon chili powder
1/4 teaspoon ground cumin

1/8 teaspoon garlic powder
3/4 cup cheddar cheese (grated)
  chips, salsa, and sour cream

PREPARATION

Simmer ingredients until steaming hot. Pour in middle of a platter surrounded by nacho chips. Serve with salsa and sour cream.

TOMATO CHEESE SPREAD

Janette Oke

■ ■ ■ ■ ■ ■ ■ ■ ■ ■ ■ ■

INGREDIENTS

$^1/_2$ can tomato soup ($^2/_3$ cup)

$^1/_2$ cup shredded American cheese

$^1/_2$ teaspoon dry mustard

$^1/_4$ teaspoon instant minced onion

PREPARATION

Cook ingredients over moderate heat, stirring constantly until cheese is melted. Chill. Serve as sandwich filling or cracker dip. Makes 1 cup.

Deb Oke with Kristie

TORTILLA AND SPINACH ROLL-UPS

Debbie Oke

INGREDIENTS

2 boxes chopped spinach
   (defrost and squeeze)
1 cup sour cream
1 can water chestnuts
   (chopped)

1 cup Miracle Whip
1 package Hidden Valley
   Ranch dressing
1 package flour tortillas
1 bottle bacon bits

PREPARATION

Combine all ingredients except bacon bits and tortillas. Spread mix on tortillas. Sprinkle with bacon bits. Roll and cut into 1-inch pieces to serve.

**What is food to one man may be
fierce poison to another.**
Lucretius

SAUSAGE STUFFED MUSHROOMS

Marvin Logan
a Favorite

■ ■ ■ ■ ■ ■ ■ ■ ■ ■ ■

INGREDIENTS

$1^1/_2$ pounds fresh medium mushrooms (about 30 large whole mushrooms)

$^1/_2$ pound pork sausage (mild)

$^1/_2$ cup mozzarella cheese (shredded)

$^1/_4$ cup seasoned bread crumbs

PREPARATION

Remove mushroom stems, carefully saving caps. Chop stems into small pieces. Brown sausage. Drain and set aside, reserving 2 tablespoons of drippings. In reserved drippings cook stem pieces over medium heat for 10 minutes. Remove from heat. Add sausage, cheese, and crumbs. Fill mushroom caps and place in ungreased 9 x 13-inch baking pan. Bake at 450°F for 8 to 12 minutes.

Daddy Marvin & Jessica Logan

2

Bars & Cookies

SUGAR COOKIES
Great Aunt Marie Ruggles

INGREDIENTS

1 pound butter or margarine
2 1/2 cups icing sugar
3 teaspoons vanilla
2 eggs

5 cups flour
1 teaspoon baking soda
1 teaspoon salt

PREPARATION

Blend butter, icing sugar, vanilla, and eggs. By hand, stir in flour, soda, and salt. Roll out 1/8-inch thick on floured surface and cut into shapes. Place on cookie sheet and sprinkle with sugar. Bake at 325°F for 10 minutes.

Nate, Jessica, & Ashley baking cookies at Grandma Janette's house

WALNUT TEA SQUARES

Aunt Marge Wiens

■ ■ ■ ■ ■ ■ ■ ■ ■ ■ ■ ■

INGREDIENTS

LOWER CRUST

3/4 cup butter

1/3 cup sugar

2 egg yolks (well beaten)

1 1/2 cups flour

1 teaspoon vanilla

UPPER CRUST

2 eggs (beaten)

2 tablespoons flour

1/4 teaspoon baking powder

1 1/2 cups brown sugar

1/2 cup walnuts (chopped)

1/4 teaspoon salt

1 teaspoon vanilla

1 cup shredded coconut
(moistened with milk)

PREPARATION

Blend ingredients for lower crust and pat into a 9 x 9-inch pan. Bake at 350°F for 12 minutes. Mix upper crust ingredients and spread over partly baked crust. Bake in moderate oven for 20 minutes. Cool and cut into squares.

Nate & Great Aunt Marge Wiens

RASPBERRY BARS

Janette Oke

■ ■ ■ ■ ■ ■ ■ ■ ■ ■ ■

INGREDIENTS

CRUST	TOPPING
1 cup flour	1 cup sugar
1 tablespoon milk	$1/4$ cup butter (melted)
1 egg	1 teaspoon vanilla
$1/2$ teaspoon salt	$1^1/2$ cups coconut
1 teaspoon baking powder	1 egg (beaten)
raspberry jam	

½ cup butter

PREPARATION

Mix as pie crust. Spread on 9 x 12-inch pan. Cover with raspberry jam. Mix topping ingredients; spread over crust and bake at 375°F for 20 minutes, or until golden brown.

DAD'S COOKIES

Janette Oke

■ ■ ■ ■ ■ ■ ■ ■ ■ ■ ■

INGREDIENTS

1 cup sugar	$1/2$ cup brown sugar

1 cup butter

1 egg (beaten)

3/4 cup coconut

1 1/2 cups flour

1 teaspoon soda

PREPARATION

Cream sugars and butter. Add beaten egg. Add dry ingredients. Form into balls and press with a glass dipped in sugar. Bake at 350°F for 15 to 18 minutes, watching carefully.

BUTTERSCOTCH SQUARES

Barbara Oke

INGREDIENTS

1 cup brown sugar

1/8 cup butter

1 egg

1 cup flour

1 teaspoon baking powder

1/4 teaspoon salt

1 teaspoon vanilla

Nuts or chips

PREPARATION

Combine ingredients and press into pan. Bake at 350°F for 20 minutes. Cool and cut into squares.

CRACKLE TOP PEANUT BUTTER COOKIES
Aunt Jean Budd

INGREDIENTS

$3/4$ cup margarine
$3/4$ cup brown sugar
1 egg (slightly beaten)
$3/4$ cup peanut butter
1 teaspoon vanilla

$13/4$ cup flour
$1/2$ teaspoon baking soda
$1/2$ teaspoon salt
$3/4$ cup sugar

PREPARATION

Cream margarine and brown sugar. Blend egg, peanut butter, and vanilla. Add flour, sifted with soda and salt. Mix well. Chill 20 to 30 minutes. Form into 1-inch balls. Roll in granulated sugar. Press and bake at 375°F for 10 to 12 minutes.

BON-BONS
Aunt June Wilson

INGREDIENTS

1-pound box powdered sugar
20 single graham crackers

(crushed)
1 cup coconut

1 cup chopped nuts

$^2/_3$ cup peanut butter (crunchy)

1$^1/_2$ sticks margarine (barely melted)

PREPARATION

Knead by hand, blending all ingredients well. Roll into balls. Place in cool place to harden. Glaze with chocolate glaze.

CHOCOLATE GLAZE

Aunt June Wilson

INGREDIENTS

1 cup chocolate chips

$^1/_3$ bar paraffin wax

PREPARATION

Heat until blended well. Dip each bon-bon into glaze. Set on waxed paper until cool and set. Store in covered canister.

Once in a young lifetime one should be allowed to have as much sweetness as one can possibly hold.
Judith Olney

CHOCOLATE MINT COOKIES

Debbie Oke

■ ■ ■ ■ ■ ■ ■ ■ ■ ■ ■ ■

INGREDIENTS

10 ounces chocolate mint chips

10 ounces chocolate chips

3³/₄ cups flour

1¹/₂ teaspoon baking soda

³/₄ teaspoon salt

1 cup butter or margarine

1¹/₂ cups sugar

³/₄ cup brown sugar

3 eggs

1¹/₂ teaspoon vanilla extract

PREPARATION

Melt 2¹/₄ cups chips (half mint and half chocolate). In small bowl combine flour, baking soda, and salt. In large bowl beat butter and sugars until creamy. Beat in melted chips, eggs, and vanilla. Gradually blend in flour mixture. Stir in remaining chips. Drop by tablespoons onto ungreased cookie sheet. Bake at 350°F for 8 to 10 minutes. Remove from oven and let stand 5 minutes. Cookies will be underbaked.

JAM THUMBPRINTS
Barbara Oke

■ ■ ■ ■ ■ ■ ■ ■ ■ ■ ■ ■ ■

INGREDIENTS

$1^1/_2$ cups flour

$^1/_4$ teaspoon salt

$^2/_3$ cup butter

$^1/_3$ cup sugar

2 egg yolks

1 teaspoon vanilla

2 egg whites (slightly beaten)

$^3/_4$ cup chopped nuts

$^1/_3$ cup raspberry or apricot jam

PREPARATION

Stir together flour and salt. In mixer bowl beat butter for 30 seconds. Add sugar and beat. Add egg yolks and vanilla. Beat well. Add dry ingredients to beaten mixture and beat until well blended. Cover and chill for 1 hour. Shape into balls. Roll in beaten egg whites and nuts and place on cookie sheet; press in thumbprint. Bake at 350°F for 15 to 17 minutes. Remove and cool. Fill centers with jam.

FRYING PAN DAINTIES
Great Aunt Laurine Steever

■ ■ ■ ■ ■ ■ ■ ■ ■ ■ ■ ■

INGREDIENTS

1¹/₂ cups chopped dates

1 cup sugar

2 eggs (beaten)

1 teaspoon vanilla

1 cup Rice Krispies

coconut or chopped nuts

PREPARATION

Put dates in frying pan. Add sugar and eggs. Mix well. Heat and keep stirring until mixture is quite thick, then remove from heat and add cereal and vanilla. Set aside to cool. Spoon out in small pieces, shape into balls, roll in coconut or chopped nuts. Wonderful for freezing.

Nate contemplating one of Grandma Janette's roses

RUBY'S COOKIES

Great-great Grandma Ruggles

■ ■ ■ ■ ■ ■ ■ ■ ■ ■ ■

INGREDIENTS

1 cup water
2 cups raisins
1 cup shortening
2 cups sugar
3 eggs
1 teaspoon vanilla
4 cups flour

1 teaspoon baking soda
1 teaspoon baking powder
1$^1/_2$ teaspoon cinnamon
$^1/_4$ teaspoon nutmeg
$^1/_4$ teaspoon allspice
pinch of salt

PREPARATION

Boil water and raisins for 5 minutes. Cool. Cream shortening and sugar. Add 3 eggs; beat well. Add vanilla, cooled raisins, flour, soda, baking powder, cinnamon, nutmeg, allspice, and salt. Mix well. Add nuts if desired. Bake in hot oven 10 to 12 minutes.

■ ■ ■ ■ ■ ■ ■ ■ ■ ■ ■

**Mighty pore bee dat don't make
mo' honey dan he want.**
Joel Chandler Harris

MOLASSES SOFTIES

Aunt Ila Steeves

■ ■ ■ ■ ■ ■ ■ ■ ■ ■ ■ ■

INGREDIENTS

$1/2$ cup melted butter or shortening
$1/2$ cup brown sugar
$1/2$ cup molasses
1 egg (beaten)
$2 1/2$ cups flour
$1/2$ teaspoon salt

1 teaspoon soda
$1/2$ cup boiling water
$1/2$ teaspoon cinnamon
$1/2$ teaspoon nutmeg
1 teaspoon vanilla
raisins (if desired)

PREPARATION

Mix butter, sugar, and molasses; add the beaten egg. Sift flour
and salt. Dissolve soda in water. Add mixture alternately with
flour. Add cinnamon, nutmeg, and vanilla. Add raisins if desired.
Drop small teaspoons of batter onto greased cookie sheet. Bake
at 350°F for 12 minutes.

REFRIGERATOR COOKIES

Aunt Betty Cox

INGREDIENTS

1 cup shortening (part butter)

$^1/_2$ cup sugar

$^1/_2$ teaspoon almond

$^1/_2$ teaspoon lemon

$^1/_2$ teaspoon vanilla

2 eggs (beaten)

1 teaspoon baking powder

$^1/_2$ teaspoon salt

$^1/_2$ cup brown sugar

$2^1/_4$ cups flour

$^1/_2$ teaspoon soda

PREPARATION

Cream shortening and add sugar. Sift together remaining dry ingredients. Add eggs and dry ingredients to shortening and sugar mixture. Roll into log shape, wrap, and chill. Slice into $^1/_8$-inch rounds. Bake at 375° to 400°F for 10 minutes.

REFRIGERATOR DATE PINWHEELS

Grandmother Mabelle Oke

■ ■ ■ ■ ■ ■ ■ ■ ■ ■ ■ ■

INGREDIENTS

2¼ cups chopped dates

1 cup sugar

1 cup water

1 cup chopped nuts

1 cup shortening

2 cups brown sugar

3 eggs (beaten)

4 cups sifted flour

½ teaspoon salt

½ teaspoon baking soda

PREPARATION

Mix dates, sugar, and water. Cook until thickened, about 10 minutes. Add walnuts and cool. Cream shortening. Add brown sugar and eggs, then remaining ingredients. Chill. Divide into 2 parts. Roll each about ¼-inch thick. Spread with half of mixture and roll up. Chill thoroughly; slice and bake at 350°F for 10 minutes.

Grandmother Mabelle Oke & Katie

3
...

Cakes & Frostings

AUNT KIT'S SOUR CREAM CAKE

Great Aunt Hazel Ruggles

■ ■ ■ ■ ■ ■ ■ ■ ■ ■ ■ ■

INGREDIENTS

3 cups flour

2 cups sugar

$^1/_4$ teaspoon baking soda

2 teaspoon baking powder

$^1/_4$ teaspoon salt

2 eggs

1 cup sour cream

1 cup sweet milk (scant)

1 teaspoon vanilla

PREPARATION

Mix flour, sugar, soda, baking powder, and salt; make nest in dry ingredients. Mix eggs, sour cream, milk, and vanilla; pour into nest. Stir until mixed. Pour into 2 8-inch cake pans and bake at 350°F for 45 to 50 minutes.

Ashley: Why waste time when eating alone? Read!

NEVER FAIL CHOCOLATE CAKE
Great Aunt Jean Ruggles Reath

■ ■ ■ ■ ■ ■ ■ ■ ■ ■ ■

INGREDIENTS

6 tablespoons cocoa

2$^1/_2$ cups flour

1$^3/_4$ cups sugar

1$^1/_4$ teaspoon baking soda

1 teaspoon baking powder

$^1/_2$ teaspoon salt

3 eggs

1 cup margarine (melted)

1$^1/_2$ cups cold water

1 teaspoon vanilla

PREPARATION

Sift first six ingredients into mixing bowl. Add remaining ingredients but do not stir until all the ingredients are in. Beat well
with electric beater. Bake in moderate oven for 40 minutes, or
until well done.

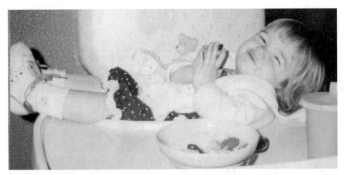

Kristie: Why waste time when eating alone? Relax!

GRANDMA RUGGLES' SPICE CAKE

Great Grandma Violet Ruggles

■ ■ ■ ■ ■ ■ ■ ■ ■ ■ ■

INGREDIENTS

1¹/₂ cups sugar

¹/₂ cup butter

1¹/₂ cups sour milk

3 eggs (separated)

2¹/₄ cups flour

1¹/₂ teaspoon allspice

¹/₂ teaspoon cloves

1 teaspoon nutmeg

1 teaspoon cinnamon

1 teaspoon baking powder

1 teaspoon baking soda

1¹/₂ cups raisins

3 egg whites

PREPARATION

Cream together sugar and butter. Add sour milk and egg yolks. In large bowl, combine dry ingredients, add slowly to wet ingredients. Fold in beaten egg whites. Bake at 350°F for 45 minutes.

Ashley in Grandma Janette's kitchen

MATRIMONIAL CAKE

Grandma Amy Steeves

■ ■ ■ ■ ■ ■ ■ ■ ■ ■ ■ ■

INGREDIENTS

1 cup butter

1 cup brown sugar

2 cups flour

1^1/$_2$ cups rolled oats

pinch salt

^{3}/$_4$ teaspoon baking soda

1 teaspoon baking powder

1 pound dates (chopped)

1 cup water

^{1}/$_2$ cup sugar

PREPARATION

Mix butter into dry ingredients. Add dates, water, and sugar. Bake in moderate oven for 45 minutes.

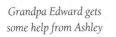

Grandpa Edward gets
some help from Ashley

BOILED RAISIN CAKE

Great Aunt Carrie Ruggles

■ ■ ■ ■ ■ ■ ■ ■ ■ ■ ■ ■

INGREDIENTS

2 eggs

2 cups brown sugar

2 cups raisins

$1/2$ teaspoon salt

$1/2$ cup shortening

2 teaspoons cinnamon

2 teaspoons cloves

2 cups hot water

2 to 3 cups flour

2 teaspoons baking soda

PREPARATION

Combine eggs, brown sugar, raisins, salt, shortening, cinnamon, and cloves; boil for 5 minutes. Cool until cold and add flour and soda. Bake in 350°F oven for 45 to 50 minutes.

■ ■ ■ ■ ■ ■ ■ ■ ■ ■ ■ ■

**If you must cry over spilt milk,
condense it.**

A. H. Hallock

MIRACLE WHIP CAKE

Great Aunt Laurine Steeves

INGREDIENTS

1 cup Miracle Whip

1 cup sugar

1 cup water

2 cups flour

6 tablespoons cocoa

dash salt

1 teaspoon vanilla

1/2 cup chopped nuts

PREPARATION

Mix together Miracle Whip, sugar, and water. In large bowl, mix remaining ingredients. Add to wet ingredients. Pour into greased pan. Bake at 350°F for 45 minutes.

**When pleasures to the eye and palate meet,
the cook has rendered his
great work complete.**
William King

CRUNCH CAKE

Debbie Oke

■ ■ ■ ■ ■ ■ ■ ■ ■ ■ ■ ■

INGREDIENTS

FIRST LAYER

1 cup graham cracker crumbs

1/2 cup nuts (chopped)

1/2 cup brown sugar (packed)

1/2 cup margarine

SECOND LAYER

1 yellow cake mix with pudding

1 cup water (or 1/2 cup water and 1/2 cup orange juice)

3 eggs

1/3 cup oil

ICING

12 ounces Cool Whip

1 tub cream cheese frosting

PREPARATION

Stir ingredients for first layer until crumbly. Put half into the bottom of 2 round, greased and floured layer cake pans. Mix second layer ingredients according to package directions. Bake at 350°F for 35 minutes. Mix cream cheese frosting and Cool Whip. Spread on cooled cake.

MY FAVORITE THINGS
Barbara Oke

■ ■ ■ ■ ■ ■ ■ ■ ■ ■ ■

INGREDIENTS

1 devils food cake mix
1 package frozen strawberries
cornstarch
1 package whipped topping
  (whipped)

1 package vanilla pudding
chocolate shavings

PREPARATION

Bake cake in bundt pan according to directions on package; let cool. Heat strawberries in saucepan and thicken with cornstarch. Drizzle over cake. Prepare pudding and whipped topping as directed on packages; mix together well. Fill center of cake with whipping cream mixture; garnish with chocolate shavings. Add extra strawberries and cream with each serving if desired.

PEANUT BUTTER PICNIC CAKE

Janette Oke—a Favorite

INGREDIENTS

1/2 cup margarine	2 teaspoons baking powder
1 1/3 cups sugar	1 teaspoon salt
1/4 cup smooth peanut butter	1 cup milk
1 teaspoon vanilla	9-ounce jar of strawberry jam
2 eggs	peanut butter frosting
2 cups all-purpose flour	

PREPARATION

Cream margarine and sugar. Add peanut butter, vanilla, and eggs; beat well. Sift together flour, baking powder, and salt. Add to creamed mixture alternately with milk, mixing well after each addition. Pour into 2 greased and floured 8- or 9-inch layer pans. Bake at 350°F for 35 to 40 minutes. Cool 10 minutes; remove from pan. Spread 2/3 cup jam between layers. Frost with peanut butter frosting.

The mother's heart is the child's schoolroom.

Henry Ward Beecher

PEANUT BUTTER FROSTING
Janette Oke

■ ■ ■ ■ ■ ■ ■ ■ ■ ■ ■

INGREDIENTS

$1/4$ cup margarine

$1/4$ cup smooth peanut butter

1 teaspoon vanilla

$1/2$ teaspoon salt

$2^1/2$ cups sifted icing sugar

3–4 tablespoons milk

PREPARATION

Cream margarine. Blend in peanut butter, vanilla, and salt. Add sugar alternately with milk. Beat until light and fluffy.

FLUFFY ICING
Aunt Betty Cox

■ ■ ■ ■ ■ ■ ■ ■ ■ ■ ■

INGREDIENTS

$1/4$ cup cold water

$3/4$ cup sugar

$1/16$ teaspoon salt

$1/8$ cream of tartar

2 teaspoons corn syrup

1 egg white

PREPARATION

Combine ingredients and beat until fluffy; cook over boiling water. Add flavoring or color.

BROWN SUGAR ICING

Aunt Joyce Deal

■ ■ ■ ■ ■ ■ ■ ■ ■ ■ ■

INGREDIENTS

2 cups brown sugar
6 tablespoons margarine
6 tablespoons cream

1 teaspoon vanilla
pinch salt

PREPARATION

Combine ingredients and boil for 2 minutes. Cool and beat until smooth (spreading consistency).

Nate "sharing" Ashley's dinner. Great Aunt Joyce Deal looks on.

RUTH YODER'S GERMAN CHOCOLATE FROSTING

Janette Oke

INGREDIENTS

1 cup evaporated milk

1 cup sugar

3 egg yolks

1/4 pound margarine

1 teaspoon vanilla

1 1/3 cups coconut

1 cup chopped pecans

PREPARATION

Cook milk, sugar, yolks, margarine, and vanilla about 12 minutes, or until it thickens. Add coconut and pecans; beat until thick.

*Jessica,
Nate with Alex,
Jackie*

ANGEL FOOD ICING
Great-great Aunt Lil Root Bly

■ ■ ■ ■ ■ ■ ■ ■ ■ ■ ■ ■

INGREDIENTS

2 teaspoons gelatin

$1/4$ cup orange juice

1 tin apricots

2 teaspoons lemon juice

$1/3$ cup sugar

1 16-ounce tin applesauce

$1/8$ teaspoon salt

1 cup whipping cream

PREPARATION

Soften gelatin in orange juice. Dissolve over boiling water (double boiler). Combine the other ingredients (except whipping cream) with gelatin. Chill until firm. Beat with beater until light and fluffy; fold in whipped cream.

Nate reads to sister Jessica

4
...
Desserts

MOM'S GOLDEN GEMS
Janette Oke

■ ■ ■ ■ ■ ■ ■ ■ ■ ■ ■ ■

INGREDIENTS

2 eggs
1 cup sugar
1 cup sweet cream
2 cups flour

1 teaspoon baking soda
   (dissolved in 1 tablespoon water)
2 teaspoons vanilla
pinch salt

PREPARATION

Lightly beat eggs. Add sugar and cream. Mix. Add remaining ingredients. Blend. Spoon into lightly greased muffin cups. Bake at 350°F for 20 to 30 minutes, or until golden. Cover with vanilla sauce.

VANILLA SAUCE (FOR GEMS)
Janette Oke

■ ■ ■ ■ ■ ■ ■ ■ ■ ■ ■ ■

INGREDIENTS

2 tablespoons butter
1 cup sugar
2 tablespoons cornstarch

1 cup hot water
2 teaspoons vanilla
1 tablespoon white vinegar

PREPARATION

In a frying pan melt butter without allowing it to bubble or scorch. Mix sugar and cornstarch; add to the melted butter, stirring to prevent burning. Add water gradually. Once smooth, allow to boil until mixture turns clear. Remove from heat and stir in vanilla and vinegar. Pour over gems and serve warm.

HASTY APPLESAUCE CRISP

Grandma Amy Steeves

INGREDIENTS

2 cups applesauce
1/4 cup butter
1/2 cup brown sugar
1 tablespoon grated orange rind

1 cup coarse graham crackers
2/3 cup chopped walnuts
nutmeg to taste

PREPARATION

Put applesauce in greased baking dish. Mix other ingredients well. Sprinkle over applesauce and bake in moderate oven for about 20 minutes. Serve hot with cream.

BAKED CUSTARD
Aunt Sharon Fehr

■ ■ ■ ■ ■ ■ ■ ■ ■ ■ ■

INGREDIENTS

3 eggs (slightly beaten)

1/4 teaspoon salt

1/3 cup sugar (or Splenda)

2 cups milk (scalded)

1/2 teaspoon vanilla

1/2 teaspoon nutmeg

PREPARATION

In a casserole dish, combine eggs, salt, and sugar. Add hot milk slowly to the egg mixture, stirring constantly. Add vanilla. Sprinkle nutmeg over top. Set the casserole dish in a pan of hot water and bake at 350°F for 50 minutes. (Or pour into 6 custard cups and bake 30 to 35 minutes.)

Variations: Add 1 cup cooked rice and 1/2 cup raisins; or 2 cups cubed bread and 1/2 cup raisins; or 2 cups cubed leftover cake. Bake as above. When cool you may use this custard for a trifle base and cover with fruit (fresh or canned, drained) and whipped cream.

R & R DESSERT

Debbie Oke
a Family Favorite

INGREDIENTS

CRUST

$1^1/_2$ sticks ($^3/_4$ cup) margarine

$^1/_2$ cup brown sugar

$1^1/_2$ cups flour

1 cup nuts (chopped)

FILLING

2 8-ounce packages cream cheese

1 cup powdered sugar

12 ounces Cool Whip (thawed)

2 small packages instant chocolate pudding

$3^1/_2$ cups milk

$^1/_3$ cup nuts (chopped)

PREPARATION

Mix crust ingredients; press into 9 x 13-inch pan; bake for 10 minutes at 350°F. Cool. Cream cheese with powdered sugar; fold in 8 ounces Cool Whip; pour onto crust. Mix pudding mixes with milk until thick; pour onto cheese/Cool Whip mixture. Top with 4 ounces Cool Whip and nuts. Refrigerate.

Variations: 1. Use banana pudding and slice 2 bananas on top of crust. 2. Use coconut pudding and top with flaked coconut. 3. Use vanilla pudding and top with cherry pie filling. 4. Use butterscotch pie filling and top with crushed heath bars.

GRAHAM DELIGHT

Debbie Oke
a Family Favorite

INGREDIENTS

2 small boxes instant vanilla
  pudding
4 cups milk

8 ounces Cool Whip (thawed)
1 box graham crackers
1 tub chocolate icing

PREPARATION

Mix pudding and milk until thick. Fold in Cool Whip. Line
9 x 13-inch pan with crackers. Pour $1/2$ pudding on crackers.
Add another layer of crackers. Pour on remainder of pudding.
Add a final layer of crackers. Top with chocolate icing. Refrigerate 24 hours.

The greatest dishes are very simple dishes.
Escoffier

STEAMED CARROT PUDDING
Great Aunt Violet Ruggles

INGREDIENTS

$1/2$ cup margarine (or 1 cup suet)

1 cup brown sugar

3 cups raisins

1 cup grated potatoes

1 cup grated carrots

$1^1/2$ cups flour

2 teaspoons baking soda

1 teaspoon salt

1 teaspoon cinnamon

1 teaspoon nutmeg

1 teaspoon allspice

PREPARATION

Mix in order given. Fill jars $3/4$ full. Steam for 3 hours. Makes about 5 quarts.

**I do not want merely to possess a faith;
I want a faith that possesses me.**
Charles Kingsley

CARAMEL PUDDING

Aunt June Wilson

■ ■ ■ ■ ■ ■ ■ ■ ■ ■ ■

INGREDIENTS

1 cup brown sugar

1 tablespoon butter

3 cups boiling water

BATTER

1 cup flour

1/2 cup raisins

1/2 cup brown sugar

2 tablespoons butter

1/2 teaspoon salt

2 tablespoons baking powder

milk (to make a stiff batter)

PREPARATION

Put 1 cup brown sugar, 1 tablespoon butter, and the water in large stove-top pudding dish; bring to a boil. Mix batter, add to first mixture as dumplings, then bake in moderately hot oven.

Nate & Jessica

RASPBERRY BAVARIAN CREAM

Barbara Oke

INGREDIENTS

¹/₄ cup sugar

7-ounce package gelatin

¹/₄ teaspoon salt

16-ounce package frozen raspberries

2 eggs (separated)

¹/₄ cup sugar

whipping cream (whipped)

1 cup raspberry preserves

PREPARATION

Combine sugar, gelatin and salt in saucepan. Add egg yolks and
raspberries. Cook over direct heat, stirring constantly, until
gelatin is dissolved (5 minutes). Remove from heat. Chill until
mixture is syrupy. Beat egg whites till soft peak forms. Gradually
add other ¹/₄ cup sugar and continue to beat until mixture
reaches stiff peaks. Fold gelatin into stiffly beaten egg whites.
Fold in whipped cream. Turn into springform pan lined with
waxed paper and chill until firm, at least 4 hours or overnight.
To serve; unmold, remove waxed paper and invert onto plate.
Warm preserves and spread over dessert.

VANILLA ICE CREAM

Aunt Ila Steeves

INGREDIENTS

2¹/₄ cups sugar
6 tablespoons flour
¹/₂ teaspoon salt
5 cups milk (scalded)

6 eggs (beaten)
4 cups heavy cream
4¹/₂ teaspoons vanilla

PREPARATION

Combine sugar, flour, and salt in saucepan. Slowly stir in hot milk. Cook over low heat for 10 minutes. Stir constantly until thickened. Mix small amount into beaten eggs. Add to hot mixture and cook 1 minute longer. Chill. Add cream and vanilla. Freeze in ice cream freezer

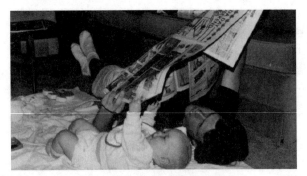

Uncle Lavon & Katie read the funnies

5
...
Egg & Cheese Dishes

EGG CHEESE CASSEROLE

Debbie Oke

INGREDIENTS

6 slices bread
butter
mustard
6 eggs
1 cup milk

salt & pepper
1 cup cheddar cheese
 (shredded)
1/3 pound ham
 (chopped or shaved)

PREPARATION

Butter bread on both sides. Place in a single layer in a 9 x 15-inch pan. Spread a thin layer of mustard over each slice. Beat eggs with fork; add milk, salt, and pepper. Pour over bread slices. Sprinkle with cheese, then lay ham over top. Cover with foil and refrigerate overnight. Bake uncovered at 350°F for 45 minutes. Cut in squares and serve hot.

**No wonder child we praise the hen,
Whose egg is mightier than the pen.**
Oliver Herford

STUFFED SHELLS
Debbie Oke

INGREDIENTS

1 pound sausage (browned and drained)

1/2 cup onion (browned with sausage)

8 ounces ricotta cheese

2 eggs (beaten)

2 cups mozzarella cheese (shredded)

1/2 cup parmesan cheese (grated)

1 teaspoon parsley flakes

1 teaspoon seasoned salt

1/4 teaspoon pepper

1 12-ounce package jumbo shells (cooked and drained)

1 30-ounce jar spaghetti sauce (or 4 cups of your favorite sauce)

1 cup mozzarella cheese (grated)

PREPARATION

Combine sausage, onion, ricotta cheese, and eggs. Stir in mozzarella, parmesan, and spices. Pour half of sauce into a 9 x 13-inch pan. Fill shells with mixture and place in baking dish. Top with remaining sauce. Sprinkle with 1 cup mozzarella. Cover. Bake at 350°F for 30 minutes. Makes 10 servings.

MACARONI AND CHEESE BAKE
Grandmother Mabelle Oke

INGREDIENTS

macaroni (cooked)   milk
cheddar cheese (grated)

PREPARATION

Grease casserole dish. Line bottom with a 1-inch layer of cooked macaroni. Spread a layer of grated cheddar cheese ½ inch thick. Continue to layer until dish is full (ending with cheese). Add milk until it is just below top. Bake at 350°F until milk cooks in and mixture thickens.

Jessica with new brother Alex

DENVER SANDWICH

Barbara Oke

INGREDIENTS

2 eggs

2 tablespoons sweet pickle relish

$1/2$ cup cooked ham (diced)

dash of salt and pepper

2 pieces of buttered toast

PREPARATION

Mix first four ingredients and scramble in a hot frying pan. Serve between toast slices.

Ashley & Courtney washing dishes at home in British Columbia

DEEP FRIED MONTEREY IN RASPBERRY SAUCE

Barbara Oke
a Family Favorite

■ ■ ■ ■ ■ ■ ■ ■ ■ ■ ■ ■

INGREDIENTS

cooking oil
  (enough to deep fry 16 2-inch
  cubes of Monterey Jack cheese)
4 eggs

3 cups fine bread crumbs
1 package frozen rasperries in
  juice
4 tablespoons cornstarch

PREPARATION

Preheat oil in deep fryer to 375°F. Dip cheese in egg and roll in bread crumbs. Chill for 15 minutes and repeat process. Chill for no less than 1 hour. Prepare sauce by heating raspberries and juice in saucepan. Add cornstarch and heat until thickened. Fifteen minutes prior to serving, drop cheese into hot oil and cook for 3 to 4 minutes. To serve, spoon ½ cup of sauce on plate and place 4 cubes on sauce. Serve hot.

6

Family Favorites

DEBBIE & LORNE OKE

Lorne and Debbie live in Mishawaka, Indiana, and have three children: Katie, Kristie, and Emily Marie. Lorne teaches at Bethel College and they coach volleyball together at the college. Debbie's parents are originally from Indiana, but she was born and raised in Kauai, Hawaii, where her parents were missionaries. Lorne and Debbie teach the young marrieds class at their church and enjoy recreational activities with their family, playing in various community leagues when possible.

FAVORITE FAMILY MEMORY

During the summer of 1993 they rode packhorses into the Canadian Rockies with Uncle "Grampa" Jack and Auntie "Grandma" Ila. Lorne had been on these types of trips several times in his younger days, but for the rest of the family it was a first. The favorite feast was the campfire breakfast. There is absolutely nothing better than "Grandma" Ila's pancakes, eggs, and bacon over an open fire.

Other favorite recipes are Nutty Baked Fish, 130; Italian Broccoli/Cauliflower Salad, 174; R & R Dessert, 57; and Graham Delight, 58.

BARBARA & TERRY OKE

Terry and Barbara have two daughters, Ashley and Courtney, and they live in Trail, British Columbia, where Terry is the administrator of an environmental organization and Barbara is the office manager for a printing company. They fill in the rest of their time with such church activities as teaching Sunday school, sponsoring youth groups, and leading singing.

FAVORITE FAMILY MEMORY

One Christmas "Grandma" Oke treated the whole family to Christmas dinner at the Banff Springs Hotel, one of Banff's oldest and finest hotels. Dressed in their best, the family arrived Christmas evening to a festival of beautiful lights, sounds, and aromas. At each place setting was a tiny gold ring holding a small scroll with the evening's menu inscribed on it. The first course was one of Barbara's favorites: oxtail soup. While watching the Marching of the Pig, an old Scottish tradition, Barbara noticed that Ashley was still perusing the menu. Then, when the waiter approached the table with steaming bowls of soup, Ashley piped up quickly but politely and asked, "Please, could I have mine with no tail." Ashley and Barbara still enjoy an occasional bowl of oxtail soup, but Barbara always makes sure her portion has the tail.

Other favorite recipes are Meatball Soup, 117; Deep Fried Monterey in Raspberry Sauce, 68; My Favorite Things, 47; and Peaches and Cream Supreme, 105.

LAVON

Lavon teaches high school music in South Bend, Indiana, and is a volunteer Young Life leader in Michiana. He enjoys being an uncle to his six nieces and two nephews and spends time with "his" kids whenever he can.

FAVORITE FAMILY MEMORY

Spending time at "Uncle Jack's house" was always a treat for Lavon. When he was about 12, he got to stay out late with his older cousins for the first time. After being pulled around the farm on a toboggan laden with cousins, the gang went out for a moonlight ice skate. The night of fun lasted past 3 a.m. A great start to many, many wonderful memories.

Lavon's favorite foods are Oke Hash (baked beans, ground beef, and rice), 129; Cheddar and Sour Cream Potatoes, 77 Grandmother Oke's Peach Ice Pie, 88; and Parmesan Layer Salad, 178.

LAUREL AND MARVIN LOGAN

Marvin and Laurel have four children who provide ample entertainment in their home. Marvin is the Engineering Manager for a company that distributes school books. Laurel homeschools their children and enjoys writing, gardening, and reading. Nate, their oldest child, enjoys computers, Nintendo, and books. Jessica enjoys being wherever she can find the biggest crowd of people or any kind of challenging activity. Jackie spends her time mothering young children or, when that opportunity is lacking, "babying" whatever animal is available. Alex keeps himself busy running, jumping, and shouting—all simultaneously.

FAVORITE FAMILY MEMORY

Many of Laurel's fondest memories center on washing dishes. After one meal she and Terry were disputing whether or not there was milk left in the pitcher, and he proved there was by dumping it on her head.

When washing dishes at Grandma Steeve's house there was never enough room for everybody, so Laurel and the younger kids mostly did legwork, gathering dishes and trying to get the clean, dried dishes put back into the cupboard before the small counter was too full to hold any more piles. There was always endless chatter and laughter.

At Grandmother Oke's house everything was orderly—a place for everything, and everything in its place—and dishes were stacked according to size and style. The kitchen was just large enough for Grandmother Oke, Mom, Aunt Alta Mae, cousin Carolyn, Laurel, an occasional male who wandered through, and lots of chatter, which was always wonderful and incredibly comfortable.

When cousin Lynn Steeves and her family stayed with the Okes for a short time, Laurel and she had their best chats over a sink full of suds. Laurel says she never feels the need for a dishwasher when she has another woman to wash dishes with.

There is something about working side by side that allows for a deep sharing of people. And there is something about the ending of a good meal, when everyone is full and relaxed, that makes it easier to be open with those around us.

Favorite dishes include Corn Chowder, 118; Sausage Stuffed Mushrooms, 24; Mom's Old Fashioned Lemon Sauce, 144; and Marv's Favorite, Sausage Apple Stuffing, 132.

7

...

Grains, Pasta, Potatoes

BUTTONS AND BOWS

Barbara Oke

■ ■ ■ ■ ■ ■ ■ ■ ■ ■ ■

INGREDIENTS

1½ cups bow-shaped pasta
2 tablespoons butter
2 tablespoons flour
½ teaspoon chicken bouillon
  mix
1 cup milk

1½ cups shredded cheddar
  cheese
4 wieners (cut into ¼-inch
  slices)
¾ cup frozen peas (thawed)
1 to 2 tablespoons ketchup

PREPARATION

Cook pasta according to package directions; drain and set aside. Melt butter in saucepan; blend in flour and bouillon mix. Gradually stir in milk. Cook and stir over medium heat until mixture comes to a boil and thickens. Remove from heat. Add cheese and stir until melted. Add wieners, peas, and ketchup. Stir over low heat until hot; do not boil. Add pasta, stirring gently to combine. Makes about 4 cups.

CHEDDAR AND SOUR CREAM POTATOES

Debbie Oke
Lavon's Favorite

INGREDIENTS

4 pounds potatoes (boiled with skins, peeled, then shredded)

1$1/2$ cups cheddar cheese (grated)

1 cup onion (chopped)

$1/4$ cup butter

1 can cream of celery soup

1 pint sour cream

$1/2$ cup Corn Flakes (crushed)

3 tablespoons butter (melted)

PREPARATION

Combine potatoes and cheddar cheese. Saute onions in $1/4$ cup butter until tender. Remove from heat; stir in soup and sour cream. Pour over potatoes and cheese, mix well. Place into a 9 x 13-inch greased pan. Cover and refrigerate overnight. Sprinkle with Corn Flakes. Drizzle with 3 tablespoons melted butter. Bake at 350°F for 1 hour.

MACARONI-BACON-TOMATO

Great Grandma Violet Ruggles

INGREDIENTS

2 cups macaroni (uncooked)

1 tin tomatoes (small)

6 to 8 slices bacon

onion (as desired, chopped)

salt and pepper

PREPARATION

Cook macaroni until tender. Drain. Add tomatoes and bacon (fry chopped bacon with onion). Add salt and pepper to taste.

Kristie discovers the pots & pans

RICE AND MUSHROOM CASSEROLE
Debbie Oke

INGREDIENTS

1¼ cups long grain rice
1¼ cups hot water
4 tablespoons onion soup mix
2 tablespoons oil

1½ tablespoons soy sauce
1 10-ounce can sliced mushrooms in liquid
1 cup frozen peas

PREPARATION

Combine first six ingredients in greased casserole dish. Cover tightly and bake for 45 minutes. Remove and stir in peas; cover and bake 15 minutes longer.

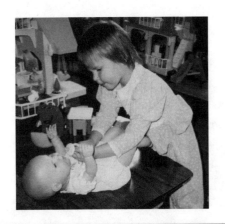

Courtney and baby doll

MANICOTTI
Barbara Oke

■ ■ ■ ■ ■ ■ ■ ■ ■ ■ ■ ■

INGREDIENTS

24 manicotti shells
1 pound hamburger
1 medium onion (chopped)
1 carton cottage cheese

1 large block mozarella cheese
 (grated)
2 jars tomato sauce

PREPARATION

Boil and prepare shells as directed. Brown hamburger and add onion. Add cottage cheese, 1 cup mozarella cheese, and $3/4$ jar of tomato sauce. Stuff into shells. Line prepared shells in casserole dish. Pour on remaining sauce and mozarella cheese. Bake at 350°F for $1/2$ hour and serve.

WHEN Laurel was learning to cook she never made anything ordinary. Her experiments ran more to things like stuffed manicotti. Some things turned out fine, but at times we longed for a nice simple meal of meat and potatoes. Always it was interesting though.

8

...

*H*oliday

CREAM NUT LOAF CANDY

Aunt Ila Steeves

■ ■ ■ ■ ■ ■ ■ ■ ■ ■ ■ ■ ■

INGREDIENTS

$1^1/_2$ cups light cream

3 cups sugar

$^1/_2$ cup syrup

$^1/_2$ tablespoon butter

1 cup walnuts (chopped)

$^3/_4$ teaspoon vanilla

PREPARATION

Boil first three ingredients until a soft ball forms when dropped into cold water. Add butter; beat until mixture thickens. Add nuts and vanilla. Pour into buttered loaf tin. Chill. Slice to serve. Note: This is the Strand family's traditional Christmas candy.

ALMOND OR PECAN CRESCENTS

Janette Oke

■ ■ ■ ■ ■ ■ ■ ■ ■ ■ ■ ■ ■

INGREDIENTS

1 cup shortening

$^1/_3$ cup sugar

$1^2/_3$ cups flour

$^1/_4$ teaspoon salt

$^2/_3$ cup chopped almonds or
     pecans

PREPARATION

Chill and roll into crescents. Dip in cinnamon and sugar. Bake at 350°F until set.

SWEET HEARTS

Janette Oke

INGREDIENTS

2¹/₄ cups unblanched almonds
3 squares (or 3 ounces)
   unsweetened chocolate
1¹/₄ cups sugar

1 teaspoon cinnamon
2 to 4 tablespoons flour
3 egg whites

PREPARATION

Grind almonds and chocolate in food grinder. Mix all other ingredients. Work with hands. Roll ¹/₄-inch thick. Cut with cookie cutter and place on sugar-covered baking sheet. Let stand 3 hours before baking. Bake at 275° for 15 to 20 minutes.

BOILED FRUITCAKE (BACHELOR'S CAKE)

Grandma Amy Steeves

INGREDIENTS

2 cups seedless raisins
1 cup brown sugar
1 cup hot water
$1/2$ cup butter
$1/2$ teaspoon salt
$1/2$ teaspoon cinnamon

$1/2$ teaspoon nutmeg
$1/4$ teaspoon cloves
$13/4$ cups flour
1 teaspoon baking soda
1 teaspoon vanilla

PREPARATION

Into a fairly large saucepan put raisins, brown sugar, hot water, butter, salt, cinnamon, nutmeg, and cloves. Bring to boiling and simmer exactly 6 minutes. Cool to lukewarm, then add flour (which has been sifted with soda). Mix well, add vanilla, and turn into cake tin lined with two thicknesses of paper. Bake in a moderate oven (325°F) for $11/2$ to 2 hours. Invert and cool in the tin. Store at least a week before cutting. Cake will remain moist for months.

EGG NOG CHEESECAKE
Barbara Oke

INGREDIENTS

1½ cups gingersnap crumbs
(approximately 30 gingersnap
cookies)

2 tablespoons brown sugar

¼ cup melted butter

FILLING

1 8-ounce package cream cheese

1 cup cottage cheese

¼ cup sugar

1 egg (separated)

1 tablespoon lemon juice

¼ cup flour

1 cup egg nog

PREPARATION

Combine cookie crumbs and sugar. Pour melted butter over crumbs and toss with a fork. Press into a greased 9-inch pie plate to form crust. In a food processor or blender, blend cheeses until smooth. Add sugar, egg, and lemon juice; blend. Add flour; blend until smooth. Pour in egg nog; blend. Pour into pie plate over crust. Bake at 325°F for 55 to 60 minutes, or until toothpick inserted comes out clean. Chill before serving. Garnish with your choice of toppings such as chocolate shavings or whipped cream.

HOLIDAY CHEESE TREE

Janette Oke

■ ■ ■ ■ ■ ■ ■ ■ ■ ■ ■ ■

INGREDIENTS

8 ounces sharp cheddar cheese
(grated)

1 8-ounce package cream
cheese (softened)

2 tablespoons finely chopped
pimento

1 teaspoon grated onion

1 tablespoon finely chopped
green pepper

1 teaspoon Worcestershire sauce

$1/2$ teaspoon lemon juice

chopped parsley

chopped nuts

PREPARATION

Combine cheeses; mix until blended. Add 1 tablespoon pimento, green pepper, onion, worcestershire sauce, and lemon juice; mix well. Chill. Drop six $1/3$-cup measures of mixture into triangle shape on serving platter. Drop remaining mixture at base of triangle; smooth to form tree. Top with parsley, nuts, and remaining pimento. Serve with Triscuit wafers.

GRANDMA'S PUMPKIN PIE
Great Aunt Violet Ruggles

■ ■ ■ ■ ■ ■ ■ ■ ■ ■ ■

INGREDIENTS

1 prepared pie crust

$1^1/_2$ cups pumpkin

1 teaspoon cinnamon

1 teaspoon nutmeg

$1/_2$ teaspoon ginger

1 tablespoon flour

1 cup sugar

$1/_4$ teaspoon salt

3 eggs

$1/_2$ cup milk

PREPARATION

Combine spices, flour, sugar, and salt with pumpkin; beat well. Beat eggs one at a time into pumpkin mixture. Add milk. Pour into pie crust. Bake in moderately hot oven. Serve with whipped cream or ice cream if desired.

Nate & friend enjoying a warm fall day

PEACH ICE PIE

Grandmother Mabelle Oke
Lavon's Favorite

■ ■ ■ ■ ■ ■ ■ ■ ■ ■ ■ ■

INGREDIENTS

1 1/4 cups water
1 package lemon or peach gelatin
1 pint vanilla ice cream

1/2 teaspoon almond extract
1 1/2 cups sliced fresh peaches
whipped cream

PREPARATION

Prepare 9-inch pie crust and bake; cool. Heat water to boiling in 2-quart saucepan. Remove from heat. Add gelatin; stir until dissolved. Add ice cream, cut into pieces and add to hot liquid. Stir until melted. Blend in almond extract. Chill until thickened but not set (25 to 35 minutes). Fold in peaches. Turn into pie shell. Chill until firm and top with whipped cream and additional peaches.

Uncle Lavon & Courtney

YULE TREE SALAD

Janette Oke

INGREDIENTS

3 packages lime-flavored gelatin
3 cups hot water
16-ounce can applesauce

1 cup slivered blanched
  almonds

PREPARATION

Seal small end of 2-quart household funnel with foil. Stand funnel in empty fruit jar, tilting slightly. Dissolve gelatin in boiling water. Divide in half and add applesauce to half and almonds to the other half. Pour $1/2$ of the applesauce mixture into tilted funnel. Chill until almost firm. Add $1/2$ of the almond mixture and tilt funnel at a different angle. Chill until almost firm. Repeat procedure with remaining gelatin to fill funnel. Then brace funnel in an upright position and chill until firm. To serve, unmold on lettuce and garnish top of tree with spiced crab apple or maraschino cherry. Makes 8 servings.

FESTIVE CANDIED YAMS

Barbara Oke

■ ■ ■ ■ ■ ■ ■ ■ ■ ■ ■ ■

INGREDIENTS

1 large yam

1 can crushed pineapple
   (drained)

1 cup pecans

$1/2$ cup brown sugar

2 teaspoons cinnamon

1 teaspoon nutmeg

20 large marshmallows

PREPARATION

Bake yam at 375°F for 45 minutes, or until soft throughout. Slice in half and scoop from peel into large bowl. Mash and add pineapple, pecans, brown sugar, cinnamon, and nutmeg. Mix well and turn into casserole dish. Bake at 350°F for 15 minutes. Remove and line marshmallows on top of yam. Return to oven and bake until marshmallows are golden brown.

9
...
International

SOT SUPPE
(SWEET SOUP)

Great Aunt Leone Edenloff

INGREDIENTS

2 quarts water

1 pound prunes

1 cup raisins

1 cup sago (minute tapioca will do)

4 tablespoons vinegar

1 1/2 cups sugar

2 cups sweetened fruit juice

1 teaspoon cloves

1 teaspoon cinnamon sticks or ground cinnamon

PREPARATION

Boil prunes and raisins until soft and plump. Add all other ingredients and simmer until sago is clear. (I usually add 2 cans of apricots or other fruit as well and use the juice as part of the sweetened fruit juice.) This is a Scandinavian dish usually served Christmas Eve.

CHICKEN CURRY (INDIAN)

Debbie Oke

INGREDIENTS

8 tablespoons butter

3 tablespoons onion (chopped)

1 teaspoon garlic

8 tablespoons flour

1 tablespoon curry powder
(or more if desired)

2 cups chicken stock

2 cups milk

salt to taste

1 stewed chicken (cut in small
pieces, boned)

PREPARATION

Melt butter; stir in onion and garlic; saute. Blend in flour and curry powder. Cook over low heat until smooth and bubbly. Remove from heat and stir in stock, milk, and salt. Stir in chicken. Simmer for 10 to 15 minutes. Serve over unsalted rice.

Condiments: Brown sugar, mango chutney, chopped peanuts, grated fresh coconut, crumbled crisp bacon. May also include sieved hard-cooked eggs or a plate of sauted bananas.

CHILDREN do not have to be very old before they express their likes and dislikes. Ours liked corn and peas and carrots. They endured beans and disliked broccoli and cauliflower. Lorne didn't care for marshmallows unless they were toasted over an open campfire, and he cheerfully forked his meringue onto someone else's plate. Laurel tried to sneak her meat under the table to the dog or casually slip unwanted dinner items down the heat register. Terry liked pie and tried, in my absence, to bake one from the freezer under the broiler. Lavon was easy to please and was always lifting the lids on the pots to sniff what was cooking.

Granddad Oke took us out to eat on occasion. One Sunday he decided to try a new Chinese restaurant. The kids were young but always enjoyed an outing. Later they asked their grandfather if we could go back to the same place again.

"You didn't even eat the food," Grandpa reminded them. "Why do you want to go back there?"

"I did too," one of them protested. "I had a Chinese hamburger."

Jackie: But we all love ice cream.

MALASADAS (OKINAWAN DOUGHNUTS)

Debbie Oke

■ ■ ■ ■ ■ ■ ■ ■ ■ ■ ■ ■

INGREDIENTS

1 package (1 tablespoon) yeast
1 teaspoon sugar
1/4 cup warm water
6 cups flour
1/2 cup sugar
1/2 teaspoon salt

1/4 cup melted butter
6 eggs
1 cup evaporated milk
1 cup water
vegetable oil for deep frying
sugar and dash of nutmeg

PREPARATION

Mix yeast with sugar and add to warm water. Let stand for 5 minutes. Sift dry ingredients together. Stir in melted butter. Beat eggs, milk, and water together; add to flour mixture. Add yeast and mix well. Dough will be sticky. Cover and let rise to double; punch down; let rise again. Heat oil to 375°F. Dip fingers in oil and pinch off golf ball size pieces of dough. Fry until one side is golden brown. Turn. Drain on towels; roll in sugar mixture. Serve immediately.

CRAB MUNDOO (KOREAN)

Debbie Oke

INGREDIENTS

1 8-ounce package cream cheese

1/4 cup Miracle Whip

1 tablespoon green onion (chopped)

1 tablespoon Worcestershire sauce

4 whole water chestnuts (optional)

8 ounces imitation crab

1 package mundoo wrappers (could use won ton wrappers)

PREPARATION

Mix first five ingredients. Place small amount on wrapper. Place some of crab on top of mixture. Dampen edges with water. Fold into a triangle and seal. Deep fry.

**Let us not go faster than God.
It is our emptiness and our thirst that he
needs, not our plentitude.**

Jacques Maritain

HANAMALU CHICKEN

Debbie Oke

INGREDIENTS

2 pounds chicken

SAUCE

1/3 cup soy sauce

2 cloves garlic (minced)

2 pieces ginger (grated)

1 teaspoon salt

4 teaspoons sugar

1 egg (crack into rest of mixture)

flour

PREPARATION

Marinate chicken in sauce ingredients. Roll in flour. Fry ahead of time (not too brown). Before serving, place in 350°F oven for 30 minutes.

**All people are made alike.
They are made of bones, flesh, and dinners.
Only the dinners are different.**

Gertrude Louise Cheney

CHILE CON QUESO
(CHEESE WITH CHILES)

Laurel Logan

INGREDIENTS

12 ounces American cheese
  (cut in cubes)
1 cup green chile salsa

2 tablespoons diced jalapenos
  (optional)
tortilla chips

PREPARATION

Combine cheese, salsa, and jalapenos. Heat until cheese is melted,
stirring occasionally. Serve hot as dip for tortilla chips.

FLAUTAS
(FLUTES)

Laurel Logan

INGREDIENTS

2 dozen small corn tortillas
FILLING
  guacamole, sour cream,
  chopped onion, sliced olives,

  shredded cheese, cilantro,
  parsley sprigs, or your choice
lettuce (shredded)
enchilada sauce (see following)

PREPARATION

Warm tortillas to soften. Overlap two tortillas for each flauta. Spoon filling down center. Roll tightly to form long tube. Secure with toothpicks. Fry in oil at 400°F until lightly browned. Drain on paper towel. Place flautas on bed of lettuce. Spoon enchilada sauce over top and garnish as desired.

ENCHILADA SAUCE

Laurel Logan

INGREDIENTS

1 cup tomato sauce
2 cups green chile salsa

$3/4$ teaspoon coriander (ground)
$1/2$ teaspoon oregano

PREPARATION

Combine all ingredients in saucepan. Simmer uncovered for 5 minutes. Spoon over main dish.

FLAN
(CARAMEL CUSTARD)

Laurel Logan

INGREDIENTS

1/2 cup sugar

4 eggs

13/4 cups milk

1/4 cup heavy cream

1/4 cup sugar

2 teaspoons vanilla

PREPARATION

Place six 6-ounce custard cups in a baking pan. Over low heat, melt sugar until lightly browned and caramelized. Immediately spoon caramelized sugar into custard cups. Cool. Beat remaining ingredients together. Pour evenly over caramel. Pour hot water to depth of 1 1/2 inches in pan around cups. Bake in 350°F oven 40 to 45 minutes or until knife inserted in custard comes out clean. Remove custard cups from pan. Cool. Refrigerate overnight. To serve, invert into dessert dish.

10
...
Jellied & Fruit Salads

AMBROSIA SALAD

Aunt Joyce Deal

■ ■ ■ ■ ■ ■ ■ ■ ■ ■ ■ ■

INGREDIENTS

8 ounces sour cream

1 tin mandarin oranges
(drained)

20-ounce tin pineapple tidbits
(drained)

1 cup fine coconut

1/2 package miniature marshmallows

PREPARATION

Mix all ingredients
together and chill over-
night.

*Alex waters
Grandma Janette's
flowers.*

FRUIT-CREAM DELIGHT

Janette Oke

■ ■ ■ ■ ■ ■ ■ ■ ■ ■ ■ ■

INGREDIENTS

$^1/_2$ cup milk (scalded)

$^1/_4$ teaspoon salt

$^1/_4$ teaspoon dry mustard

4 egg yolks (well beaten)

juice of 1 lemon

2 cups whipping cream

$^1/_3$ cup powdered sugar

1 pound miniature marshmallows

1 cup chopped pecans

14-ounce can white pitted cherries (drained)

14-ounce pineapple tidbits (drained)

lettuce leaves

PREPARATION

Add seasonings to milk. Pour slowly into well-beaten egg yolks. Cook in double boiler or over very low heat, stirring constantly, until mixture coats spoon. Remove from heat immediately and cool. Add lemon juice. Whip cream and beat in powdered sugar. Gently fold in cooled custard, marshmallows, nuts, and well-drained cherries and pineapple. Chill overnight. Serve in lettuce-lined bowl or individual lettuce cups. Serves 8 to 10.

24-HOUR SALAD
Great Aunt Violet Ruggles

■ ■ ■ ■ ■ ■ ■ ■ ■ ■ ■ ■

INGREDIENTS

2 eggs (beaten)

4 tablespoons vinegar

4 tablespoons sugar

2 tablespoons butter

1 cup cream (whipped)

2 cups grapes (halved)

2 cups pineapple (cut in pieces)

2 oranges (peeled, sectioned, and cut—or 2 cans mandarins)

2 cups miniature marshmallows

PREPARATION

Put eggs in double boiler and add vinegar and sugar, beating constantly until smooth. Remove from heat. Add butter and cool. When cool, fold in whipped cream. Add fruit and marshmallows. Refrigerate for 24 hours before serving.

DURING my childhood, a glass footed-bowl identified an event as being special. It was always filled with sparkling, colorful jello for special meals. The bowl had been given to my mother for her sixteenth birthday by a dear neighbor from her own cupboard of dishes. No one knows its age.

Christmas, Easter, and other special occasions were graced by the footed-bowl. It passed from one fumbling

PEACHES AND CREME SUPREME

Barbara Oke

INGREDIENTS

1 large package peach gelatin
1 can peaches (drained)

1 small carton whipping cream
(whipped)

PREPARATION

Prepare gelatin according to package directions. Set aside 1 cup of liquid and chill remainder until slightly thickened. Mix cup of remaining liquid with whipped cream; pour into mold; chill until set. Mix thickened liquid with peaches and pour into mold. Chill until set; unmold and serve.

pair of childish hands to another, round and round our kitchen table. The jello—whether cherry red, lemon yellow, or shimmering orange—was always topped with rich, thick, farm whipped-cream. Sometimes the Jello bore fruit or nuts and sometimes it was plain—but always it was greatly enjoyed. When the footed dish of jello appeared at the table, we knew the meal was a special one.

ORANGE-CREAM CHEESE SALAD LOAF

Janette Oke

■ ■ ■ ■ ■ ■ ■ ■ ■ ■ ■ ■

INGREDIENTS

11-ounce can mandarin orange
  sections (drained)
6-ounce package gelatin
  (orange- or lime-flavored)
1$^1/_2$ cups boiling water

1 cup orange juice
ice cubes
8-ounce package cream cheese
  (softened)

PREPARATION

Arrange orange sections in a 9 x 5-inch loaf pan. Dissolve gelatin in boiling water. Combine juice and ice cubes to make 2$^1/_2$ cups. Add to gelatin and stir until slightly thickened; remove any unmelted ice. Measure 1 cup gelatin; blend into softened cream cheese. Pour remaining gelatin over orange sections in pan. Top with creamy mixture. Chill 4 hours or overnight. Makes 12 servings.

11

Kids' Stuff

CONE-CUPS

Janette Oke

INGREDIENTS

flat-bottomed cone cups | cake batter

PREPARATION

Youngsters love cup-cakes. And they love to make them as well as eat them. Cone-cups are a fun treat. Fill flat-bottom ice cream cones half full of cake batter and bake in a slow oven on a cookie sheet. Serve plain or iced. They're great to have along on a car trip for a snack (no crumbly cupcake liners are left over).

Katie, Nate, Jessica, & Jackie enjoy a picnic on Grandma Janette's porch.

CARAMEL POPCORN

Aunt Betty Cox

■ ■ ■ ■ ■ ■ ■ ■ ■ ■ ■

INGREDIENTS

2 cups brown sugar

$1/2$ pound margarine

$1/2$ cup corn syrup
   (Roger's Golden in Canada)

$1/2$ teaspoon salt

1 teaspoon baking soda

28 to 32 cups popped corn

PREPARATION

Boil sugar, margarine, syrup, and salt for 5 minutes (soft ball stage). Add soda and stir well. Pour over popped corn (peanuts optional). Bake in 200°F oven for 1 hour stirring every 15 minutes.

■ ■ ■ ■ ■ ■ ■ ■ ■ ■ ■

**When I was a kid my mother always offered
me two choices at supper: Take it or leave it.**

Sam Levenson

PLAY DOUGH

Debbie Oke

INGREDIENTS

2 cups flour

1 cup salt

2 tablespoons cream of tartar

2 cups water

2 tablespoons oil

food coloring (several drops)

PREPARATION

Mix dry and liquid ingredients separately. Combine and stir over medium heat until mixture pulls away from pan. Cool a few minutes then knead. Store in air tight container. Will keep for 6 to 7 months. Hints: 1 or 2 drops of cinnamon, peppermint, or wintergreen oil may be added for a refreshing smell. If you wish to make several colors, add coloring just before kneading.

GIANT BUBBLES

Debbie Oke

INGREDIENTS

6 cups water

2 cups Joy dishwashing liquid

$3/4$ cup light corn syrup

PREPARATION

Mix well and let sit for 4 hours before use. Use a large store bought wand or make one out of a coat hanger. Be sure to bend back sharp ends to avoid points that would pop the bubble. Pour mix into a shallow pan and enjoy!

MY mother was creative as well as patient, but I didn't realize just how patient until I tried to copy one of her ideas.

At Easter my mother often made a special Easter basket consisting of jello Easter eggs nestled on a plate of whipped cream that had been sprinkled with green-colored coconut. For several weeks before Easter she "blew" eggs out of their shells whenever she needed one for baking. Then she rinsed the shells and carefully taped the bottoms. When Easter arrived she filled each eggshell with jello until she had orange, yellow, green, and various shades of red eggs. They were made much like a finger jello of today. The eggs were quickly dipped in hot water and peeled and placed in their whipped-cream nest. We loved them, but I didn't fully appreciate the work that went into them until I prepared them for my own children.

Ashley & Courtney making Easter eggs

COAL PORT MIXTURE
(FOR PLAQUES OR MOLDS)

Janette Oke

■ ■ ■ ■ ■ ■ ■ ■ ■ ■ ■ ■

INGREDIENTS

1 egg white (slightly beaten)
1 cup bread crumbs without
   crusts
1 cup water

1 cup flour
2 tablespoons salt
1 tablespoon alum

PREPARATION

Mix all ingredients together until mixure looks like pie dough.

BABY WIPES

Debbie Oke

■ ■ ■ ■ ■ ■ ■ ■ ■ ■ ■ ■

INGREDIENTS

paper towels
2 tablespoons baby oil

2 tablespoons baby shampoo
2 cups hot water

PREPARATION

Cut towels in half. Place in appropriately sized airtight container
or ziploc bag. Mix liquid ingredients and pour over towels.

12
...
Lunch Ideas

PRONTO PUPS
Aunt Joyce Deal

■ ■ ■ ■ ■ ■ ■ ■ ■ ■ ■ ■ ■

INGREDIENTS

1 cup flour

$1/4$ cup sugar

1 egg

1 teaspoon salt

$2/3$ cup cornmeal

1 cup milk (or less)

3 teaspoons baking powder

wieners

PREPARATION

Mix well. Dip wiener in batter and deep fry 4 to 5 minutes.

WAFFLED SANDWICHES
Debbie Oke

■ ■ ■ ■ ■ ■ ■ ■ ■ ■ ■ ■ ■

INGREDIENTS

white bread slices

butter

thin apple slices

cooked bacon slices

American cheese slices

PREPARATION

Butter bread on outside. Layer with 4 apple slices, 3 bacon slices, and 1 slice cheese. Grill in waffle iron until lightly browned.

UNCLE JIM'S SPECIALTY
Great Aunt Jean Ruggles Reath

INGREDIENTS

2 slices brown bread (toasted)
mayonnaise
Cheez Whiz

sliced tomatoes
4 slices crisp bacon
1 onion (thinly sliced)

PREPARATION

Spread one slice of toast with mayonnaise and the other slice with Cheese Whiz (no butter or margarine needed). Arrange tomato slices, adding salt and pepper if desired. Add onion and bacon. Add top slice of toast.

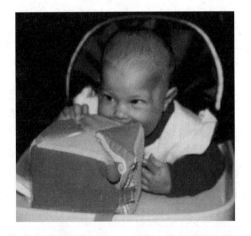

Ashley tries solid food

CREAM OF BROCCOLI CHOWDER

Grandmother Mabelle Oke

■ ■ ■ ■ ■ ■ ■ ■ ■ ■ ■ ■

INGREDIENTS

3 potatoes (cut in cubes)

1 large onion

1 bunch broccoli (chopped)

1 carrot (grated)

3 celery ribs

3 cups water

1 teaspoon (2 cubes) Chicken-in-a-Mug

1 teaspoon salt

1/4 teaspoon pepper

1 cup grated cheese

SAUCE

1 quart milk

1/2 cup flour

1/2 cup margarine

PREPARATION

Cook vegetables in water. Make white sauce and add the cooked vegetables to the sauce (do not boil after adding vegetables to sauce). Add grated cheese and simmer a few minutes before serving.

MEATBALL SOUP

Barbara Oke

INGREDIENTS

1 pound hamburger
1 egg
$^1/_2$ cup fine bread crumbs
1 tablespoon Maggi seasoning
1 teaspoon pepper

6 cups beef stock
celery (finely chopped)
vegetable soup mix
vermicelli
salt and pepper to taste

PREPARATION

Mix hamburger, egg, bread crumbs, Maggi, and pepper. Roll into bite-sized balls. Heat beef stock to boiling; add celery, soup mix, and meat balls. Break vermicelli into small pieces and add to soup (as much as desired). Simmer for $^1/_2$ hour. Add salt, pepper, and Maggi to taste.

CORN CHOWDER

Marvin Logan
a Family Favorite

INGREDIENTS

¹/₄ cup chopped onions

2 tablespoons margarine

3 tablespoons flour

1¹/₂ cups milk

1 can kernel corn (drained)

¹/₂ cup water

salt and pepper to taste

PREPARATION

Saute onions in margarine. Add flour; stir until no lumps remain. Add milk slowly, stirring until smooth. Add corn to mixture. Heat on medium until boiling. Add water slowly, reduce to simmering. Simmer 15 minutes; add salt and pepper to taste.

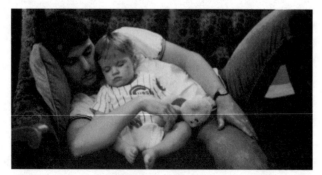

Daddy Marvin & Nate

13

...

Main Dishes

MEATBALL CASSEROLE

Janette Oke

■ ■ ■ ■ ■ ■ ■ ■ ■ ■ ■ ■

INGREDIENTS

ground beef

minced onion (divided)

1 can cream of mushroom soup

1 can cream of chicken soup

1 can water

soy sauce

$1/3$ cup Minute Rice (brown)

1 cup frozen peas

whole wheat crackers (crushed)

cheddar cheese (grated)

PREPARATION

Mix ground beef with onions, salt, and pepper. Form into meatballs. Cook in frying pan until well done. Add soups, water, onion, soy, Minute Rice, and peas. Place in buttered casserole dish. Bake at 350°F for 30 minutes (longer if mixture has cooled). Sprinkle top with crushed whole wheat crackers, followed by grated cheddar cheese. Bake for an additional 5 to 10 minutes or until cheese has melted.

PORK OF THREE KINGDOMS

Barbara Oke

INGREDIENTS

pork (cubed)

BATTER

2 cups flour

$1/2$ cup milk

1 teaspoon cinnamon

1 tablespoon baking powder

2 eggs

salt and pepper

1 teaspoon nutmeg

$1/4$ teaspoon cornstarch

SAUCE

1 teaspoon ketchup

$3/4$ cup vinegar

2 tablespoons lemon juice

$3/4$ cup brown sugar

$3/4$ cup water

PREPARATION

Dip cubes of pork into batter and deep fry till golden brown. Place in baking dish. Bring sauce ingredients to boil and add cornstarch to thicken; pour sauce over pork. Bake at 350°F for $1/2$ hour. Serve with rice.

PORCUPINES

Aunt Marge Wiens

■ ■ ■ ■ ■ ■ ■ ■ ■ ■ ■

INGREDIENTS

2 tins (cans) tuna

$1/2$ cup uncooked rice

$1/2$ cup grated raw carrot

2 tablespoons finely chopped
   onion

1 medium egg

$1/2$ teaspoon salt

pepper

1 can cream of mushroom soup

$1/2$ cup water

PREPARATION

Mix together tuna with liquid, rice, carrots, onion, and egg. Season with salt and pepper. Shape into balls. Place in buttered dish, leaving space for expansion during cooking. Mix soup and water. Pour over all. Cover dish. Bake in moderate oven for 1 hour.

■ ■ ■ ■ ■ ■ ■ ■ ■ ■ ■

**We can't form our children on our own
concepts; we must take them and love them
as God gives them to us.**

Goethe

FRENCH FRIED FISH

Aunt Betty Cox

INGREDIENTS

2 eggs (separated)

$^2/_3$ cup milk

2 tablespoons lemon juice

1 tablespoon salad oil

1 teaspoon salt

1 cup flour

PREPARATION

Beat egg whites. Fold into other mixed ingredients. Dip fish. Cook in oil at 370°F about 7 minutes.

Grandpa Edward with Nate & Ashley

SALMON PIE
Aunt Sharon Fehr

■ ■ ■ ■ ■ ■ ■ ■ ■ ■ ■

INGREDIENTS

2 cups canned salmon

1/2 cup sandwich spread or tartar sauce

1/4 cup margarine (melted)

2 tablespoons vinegar (scant)

1/2 teaspoon salt

1/4 teaspoon pepper

1 teaspoon Worcestershire sauce

3 cups soft bread crumbs

PREPARATION

In first bowl mix salmon and sandwich spread with a fork. In second bowl mix margarine, vinegar, salt, pepper, and worcestershire sauce. In third bowl place bread crumbs. Add enough melted margarine mixture to just moisten. Toss lightly with a fork. Pat half of the crumb mixture into the bottom of a pie plate. Spread salmon on top. Cover with remaining crumb mixture. Drizzle rest of margarine mixture over crumbs. Bake at 400°F for 15 minutes, or until crumbs brown. Serve with a tossed salad.

SEAFOOD STROGANOFF

Barbara Oke

INGREDIENTS

1 1/2 pound fish fillets (thawed
  or fresh)

1/4 cup butter or margarine

1 large onion (thinly sliced)

1 1/2 cups sliced mushrooms

1/4 cup cider vinegar

1 teaspoon salt

dash pepper

1 teaspoon Worcestershire sauce

1/2 teaspoon mustard

1 1/2 cups sour cream

hot cooked noodles

juice of 1/2 lemon

PREPARATION

Cut fish into 1/2-inch strips. Saute onion in butter until tender; stir in mushrooms and cook until tender. Set aside. Saute fish in same pan about 4 minutes, or until flesh flakes easily. Stir gently. Combine remaining ingredients (except noodles and lemon juice) and add to pan with mushroom and onion; heat. Serve over hot cooked noodles; drizzle with lemon juice. Note: cod, sole, halibut, perch, or char are best.

BAKED CHICKEN WITH CREAM

Great Grandma Violet Ruggles

INGREDIENTS

chicken pieces
flour

salt and pepper to taste
2 cups cream

PREPARATION

Roll each chicken piece in flour and place in casserole dish. Add salt and pepper; pour 2 cups of cream over top. Cover tightly and bake until chicken is tender and turns a rich brown.

FRIED CHICKEN

Grandma Amy Steever

INGREDIENTS

chicken pieces
flour
butter (melted)

salt & pepper
cream

PREPARATION

Roll chicken pieces in flour to coat. Place chicken in frying pan with ample melted butter. Brown on all sides. Place in oven pan

with lid (add a small amount of water so chicken will steam).
For the last few minutes of cooking pour cream over chicken.

CHICKEN ALA CRESCENTS

Debbie Oke

■ ■ ■ ■ ■ ■ ■ ■ ■ ■ ■ ■

INGREDIENTS

8 chicken breasts (cooked and
  cut into bite-sized pieces)
8-ounce package and 3-ounce
  package cream cheese
6 tablespoons butter (melted)
3 tablespoons lemon-pepper
  seasoning
4 ounces canned mushrooms

3 packages crescent rolls
GRAVY
$3/4$ cup butter (melted)
1 cup Italian croutons (crushed)
$1/2$ cup pecans (crushed)
1 cup broth
1 can mushroom soup

PREPARATION

Blend cream cheese, butter, and seasoning. Combine with mushrooms and chicken pieces. Roll each package of crescent rolls
into 8 rectangles (approximately 3 x 4 inches). Fill each with 2
tablespoons chicken mixture. Roll up and seal. Dip each roll into
butter; roll in croutons and pecans. Bake at 375°F for 25
minutes. Make gravy with broth and soup. Thicken if desired.

LENTIL STEW
Aunt Sharon Fehr

INGREDIENTS

1 cup dried lentils (rinsed)

$4^1/_2$ cups water

5 teaspoons Beef-in-a-Mug (or
   2 beef bouillon cubes)

1 bay leaf (I put it in a tea ball)

2 teaspoons salt

$^1/_2$ pound diced ham (or leftover meat)

1 can tomato soup

$^1/_8$ teaspoon oregano

1 onion (chopped)

2 stalks celery (chopped)

1 clove garlic (minced, optional)

PREPARATION

Bring lentils, water, Beef-in-a-Mug, bay leaf, and salt to a boil; simmer 20 minutes. Add ham, tomato soup, oregano, onion, celery, and garlic. Bring to a boil. Reduce heat and simmer 20 to 30 minutes. Remove bay leaf. Serve with a whole grain bread.

**Strange to see how a good dinner and feasting
reconciles everybody.**

Samuel Pepys

OKE HASH
(BEAN AND BEEF STOVE-TOP CASSEROLE)

Janette Oke
Lavon's Favorite

INGREDIENTS

1 pound lean ground beef

1 tablespoon onion (chopped)

1 can pork and beans

1 can water

$1/3$ cup Minute Rice

ketchup (to taste)

salt and pepper

PREPARATION

Brown beef with chopped onions. Add remaining ingredients. Simmer until rice is tender.

Uncle Lavon & Ashley

NUTTY BAKED FISH

Debbie Oke

INGREDIENTS

1 pound orange roughy or any
  mild white fish
1 tablespoon lemon juice
salt and pepper
2 tablespoons butter

1 cup almonds
$1/2$ teaspoon cinnamon
$1/4$ cup milk
4 ounces Monterey Jack cheese
2 to 3 tablespoons bread crumbs

PREPARATION

Place fillets in greased baking dish. Brush with lemon juice;
sprinkle with salt and pepper. In a food processor, combine
remaining ingredients except bread crumbs. Process until finely
chopped. Spread over fish. Sprinkle with bread crumbs. Bake at
400°F for 20 to 30 minutes, or until fish flakes. May broil for 1
minute to brown slightly.

**A man is in general better pleased when he
has a good dinner upon his table than when
his wife talks Greek.**

Dr. Johnson

BEEF 'N' POTATO BAKE

Laurel Logan

INGREDIENTS

4 cups frozen hash brown potatoes (thawed)

3 tablespoons oil

1/4 teaspoon pepper

1 pound ground beef

3/4-ounce package brown gravy
  mix

1 cup water

1/2 teaspoon garlic salt

10-ounce package mixed frozen
  vegetables

1 cup shredded cheddar cheese

canned french fried onion rings

PREPARATION

In shallow 1 1/2 quart baking dish, combine potatoes, oil, and pepper. Press firmly to bottom and sides of dish. Bake shell uncovered at 400°F for 15 minutes. Brown beef and drain. Add gravy mix, water, and garlic salt. Bring to slow boil. Add vegetables and cook on medium for 5 minutes. Add 1/2 cup cheese; place into potato shell. Bake uncovered at 350°F for 15 minutes. Sprinkle with remaining cheese and onion rings; return to oven for 5 minutes.

SAUSAGE APPLE STUFFING

Laurel Logan
Marv's Favorite

■ ■ ■ ■ ■ ■ ■ ■ ■ ■ ■ ■

INGREDIENTS

1 pound mild pork sausage
1 tablespoon margarine
1 cup diced apple (peeled)
1 medium onion (diced)

$1/4$ cup apple juice
2 cups bread crumbs for stuffing
$1/2$ teaspoon pepper
$1/2$ teaspoon poultry seasoning

PREPARATION

Brown sausage and set aside. Saute apple and onion in margarine. Add apple juice, bread crumbs, seasonings, and sausage. Stuff into a bird or bake in greased dish at 350°F for 30 minutes.

Jessica,
Nate with Alex,
Jackie

14

...

Nuts & Berries

(and other healthy stuff)

HEALTH MUFFINS

Janette Oke

INGREDIENTS

natural grains (bran, oatmeal,
  wheat, cornmeal, etcetera, in
  any combination)
1 tablespoon baking powder
3 ripe mashed bananas

1 can unsweetened applesauce
$1/3$ cup molasses
$1/4$ cup any unsweetened fruit
  juice

PREPARATION

Blend grains. Add remaining ingredients. Dough should be firm
but well moistened. Fill greased muffin cups $2/3$ full. Bake at
375°F for 25 to 30 minutes.

VARIATIONS

change grain combinations
add chopped fruit such as
  raisins or currants
add nuts (chopped) or trail mix

add crunchy cereal
add chippits (any flavor)
spice

LOWFAT BRAN MUFFINS
Debbie Oke

INGREDIENTS

1 cup flour

2 teaspoons baking powder

$1/2$ teaspoon baking soda

$1/2$ teaspoon cinnamon

2 cups 100% bran

$1^1/_4$ cups 2% lowfat milk

$1/3$ cup brown sugar (packed)

1 egg

$1/2$ cup applesauce

PREPARATION

In large bowl, mix flour, baking powder, soda, and cinnamon. In medium bowl, mix cereal, milk, and sugar; let stand 5 minutes. Stir in egg and applesauce. Add to flour mixture, stirring just until moistened. Fill each cup $2/3$ full. Bake in a greased muffin tin at 400°F for 18 to 20 minutes.

Nutritional information: 120 calories, 2 g fat, 20 mg cholesterol, 200 mg sodium, 5 g dietary fiber.

GRANOLA

Aunt Joyce Deal

■ ■ ■ ■ ■ ■ ■ ■ ■ ■ ■ ■

INGREDIENTS

3 cups rolled oats

1 cup bran

1 cup sesame seeds

1 cup wheat germ

1 cup brown sugar

1 cup nuts

1 cup raisins

$1/4$ cup salad oil

vanilla

$1/2$ cup honey

PREPARATION

Mix together. Bake at 250°F for 1 hour. Stir 3 times during baking.

SMOOTHIES

Debbie Oke

■ ■ ■ ■ ■ ■ ■ ■ ■ ■ ■ ■

INGREDIENTS

1 cup apple juice

1 banana

5 frozen strawberries

PREPARATION

Blend ingredients in blender until smooth. Try different juices and frozen fruit.

MUSHROOM BARLEY SOUP
Debbie Oke

■ ■ ■ ■ ■ ■ ■ ■ ■ ■ ■ ■

INGREDIENTS

2 large yellow onions (chopped)

3 medium carrots (sliced)

2 stalks celery

1/2 pound mushrooms (sliced thin)

4 cups beef broth

1/4 cup chopped parsley

1/2 cup medium-size barley

1/4 teaspoon pepper

salt to taste

PREPARATION

Place all ingredients in pan and boil for 4 minutes. Simmer partly covered for 40 minutes or until the barley is tender. Serves 4.

■ ■ ■ ■ ■ ■ ■ ■ ■ ■ ■ ■

Lord, this humble house we'd keep
Sweet with play and calm with sleep.
Help us so that we may give
Beauty to the lives we live.
Let Thy love and let Thy grace,
Shine upon our dwelling place.

Edgar A. Guest

LOW-CAL SPAGHETTI PIE
Laurel Logan

■ ■ ■ ■ ■ ■ ■ ■ ■ ■ ■ ■

INGREDIENTS

2 cups thin spaghetti

$1/4$ cup grated parmesan cheese

1 egg (beaten)

$1^1/2$ teaspoons margarine (softened)

$2/3$ cup ricotta cheese

2 teaspoons margarine

$1/2$ cup diced onion

$1/2$ cup red or green bell pepper

1 clove garlic (minced)

$1/2$ pound ground beef

1 cup canned whole tomatoes (chopped)

$1/4$ cup tomato paste

$1/4$ cup shredded mozzarella cheese

PREPARATION

Combine the first four ingredients. Spray pie plate with no-stick spray and arrange spaghetti mixture to form shell. Spread ricotta cheese over bottom of shell. Brown ground beef; drain and set aside. Saute onion, pepper, and garlic in margarine. Add beef, tomatoes, and paste. Cook until bubbly and thickened. Spoon over ricotta cheese and bake at 350°F for 20 to 25 minutes. Sprinkle with mozzarella cheese for last 5 minutes of baking time. Remove from oven and let stand about 5 minutes before serving.

15...

_O_ ver Top

_Sauces & spreads to top
all kinds of foods_

RHUBARB MARMALADE

Grandma Amy Steeves

■ ■ ■ ■ ■ ■ ■ ■ ■ ■ ■ ■

INGREDIENTS

6 quarts washed, chopped
  rhubarb

6 oranges
12 cups sugar

PREPARATION

Mix prepared rhubarb with whole oranges processed through food grinder. Mix in sugar. Cook slowly in large kettle (makes own juice). Cook until desired consistency. Bottle in sterilized jars and seal.

Ashley & Teddies

STRAWBERRY JIFFY JAM

Janette Oke

INGREDIENTS

2 cups washed and hulled strawberries

1 cup cold water

3-ounce package strawberry-flavored gelatin

PREPARATION

Crush strawberries in a saucepan. Add water and strawberry gelatin. Heat mixture to boiling over medium heat, stirring constantly. Lower heat; simmer 2 minutes. Pour into jars; cover. Store in refrigerator.

VARIATION

Sugar-Free Strawberry Jiffy Jam: Heat 2 cups crushed strawberries in 2 cups water to boiling. Remove from heat; stir in one 4-serving envelope (1/2 package) low-calorie strawberry-flavored gelatin. Stir until thoroughly dissolved. (Three calories per tablespoon.)

RICH CUSTARD SAUCE

Janette Oke

■ ■ ■ ■ ■ ■ ■ ■ ■ ■ ■ ■ ■

INGREDIENTS

2 eggs (slightly beaten)
$2/3$ cup sweetened condensed
  milk
$1 1/2$ cups water

$1/4$ teaspoon salt
1 teaspoon vanilla
$1/2$ cup heavy cream

PREPARATION

Combine eggs, condensed milk, water, and salt in a medium-size heavy saucepan. Cook over low heat, stirring constantly, until mixture is thickened and coats a metal spoon, about 10 minutes. Remove from heat; add vanilla. Refrigerate until cold. Just before serving, whip cream until stiff; fold into chilled custard. Serve over fresh strawberries, other fresh fruit, drained canned fruit, or puddings.

Note: If using a lightweight saucepan, cook custard over hot, not boiling, water. Cooking time will be longer.

BUTTERSCOTCH SAUCE

Janette Oke

INGREDIENTS

1 cup light corn syrup
1 cup brown sugar
salt

1/2 cup milk
3 tablespoons butter
vanilla

PREPARATION

Bring ingredients to full boil. Cook 5 more minutes. Makes 1 pint.

BLANC MANJE

Barbara Oke

INGREDIENTS

6 tablespoons cornstarch
1/4 cup sugar

pinch salt
4 cups milk

PREPARATION

Combine first 3 ingredients. Add some milk to make paste. Add milk and bring to boil. Add flavor and cool. Pour in dishes or over fresh fruit.

MOM'S OLD FASHIONED LEMON SAUCE
Laurel Logan
a Family Favorite

INGREDIENTS

1 cup sugar

$^1/_2$ cup butter or margarine

$^1/_4$ cup water

1 egg (well beaten)

$^3/_4$ teaspoon finely grated lemon

3 tablespoons lemon juice

PREPARATION

Combine all ingredients in saucepan. Heat to boiling over medium heat, stirring constantly. Serve warm over cake, ice cream, or sweet breads.

Jackie playing with farm kitten

16
...
Pies & Crusts

PIE CRUST

Janette Oke

■ ■ ■ ■ ■ ■ ■ ■ ■ ■ ■ ■

INGREDIENTS

6 cups flour (more if needed)
2 cups lard
1 cup margarine
1 teaspoon baking powder

3/4 teaspoon salt
1 1/2 cups ice water (may not
    need it at all)

PREPARATION

Mix lard and margarine with flour, baking powder, and salt. Add enough water to handle well. Makes approximately 5 crusts.

Ashley at Grandma Janette's baking an apple pie for Daddy

WALNUT CRUST

Janette Oke

■ ■ ■ ■ ■ ■ ■ ■ ■ ■ ■ ■

INGREDIENTS

1 cup butter or margarine

$1/3$ cup sugar (white or brown)

3 cups all-purpose flour

10 ounces ($2^3/_4$ cups) walnuts or pecans (chopped fine or ground)

1 egg (slightly beaten)

1 teaspoon grated rind from a citrus fruit

1 teaspoon vanilla extract

PREPARATION

Cream butter and sugar. Add remaining ingredients. Mix well. Press into two greased pans. Build up the edge. Bake at 350°F for 10 to 12 minutes. Crusts may be frozen. Note: Recipe may be halved; or bake one pie shell and freeze remaining crumb mixture. Makes two 9-inch pie crusts.

■ ■ ■ ■ ■ ■ ■ ■ ■ ■ ■ ■

Who will deny the truth?
There is poetry in pies.
Henry Wadsworth Longfellow

KEY LIME PIE

Janette Oke

■ ■ ■ ■ ■ ■ ■ ■ ■ ■ ■ ■ ■

INGREDIENTS

1 1/2 cups graham wafer crumbs
1/3 cup brown sugar
1/8 teaspoon salt
5 tablespoons butter (melted)
3 eggs (separated)

1 1/3 cups (1 can) sweetened
   condensed milk
1/2 cup lime juice
green food color

PREPARATION

Preheat oven to 350°F. Mix crumbs, sugar, salt, and butter together. Reserve 1/4 cup crumb mixture for garnish. Place remaining crumb mixture into a buttered, 9-inch pie plate and press firmly onto bottom and sides. Beat egg yolks until thick and light; stir in milk, lime juice, and enough green food coloring to give a natural lime tint. Sprinkle egg whites with a few grains of salt and beat until stiff but not dry. Add to lime mixture and fold in gently to combine. Turn into prepared pie shell and sprinkle with 1/4 cup crumbs. Bake for about 25 minutes. Cool at room temperature. For extra richness, omit crumbs on top of pie and garnish with whipped cream at serving time.

SIX-MINUTE PECAN PIE
Aunt Marge Wiens

INGREDIENTS

3 eggs (slightly beaten)
1 cup corn syrup
1 cup sugar
2 tablespoons butter or
  margarine

1 teaspoon vanilla
$1\frac{1}{2}$ cups pecans
1 unbaked pie shell

PREPARATION

In large bowl stir together first five ingredients until well blended.
Stir in nuts. Pour into pastry shell. Bake in 350°F oven 50 to 55
minutes, or until knife inserted halfway between center and edge
comes out clean. Cool.

Nate shares with Grandpa Edward

CUSTARD PIE

Great-great Grandma Amy Elizabeth Passon Ruggles

INGREDIENTS

1 quart milk

2 eggs

3 tablespoons sugar

PREPARATION

Line a $1\frac{1}{2}$-inch pie tin with crust and set on stove for a minute to cook the crust. Heat milk to boiling. Beat eggs with sugar; flavor to taste. Add milk. Turn into crust and bake just until firm. If some cream is used it is an improvement.

*Great-great Grandmother
Amy Elizabeth Passon Ruggles*

SHORTBREAD PUMPKIN PIE
Debbie Oke

INGREDIENTS

CRUST

1 cup butter or margarine

$1/_2$ cup sugar

3 cups flour

FILLING

$3^1/_2$ cups pumpkin
  (29-ounce can)

$3^1/_2$ cups evaporated milk

$1^1/_2$ cups sugar

4 eggs

1 teaspoon salt

1 teaspoon cinnamon

1 teaspoon ginger

1 teaspoon cloves

PREPARATION

Cream butter and sugar for crust. Add flour and mix well. Press firmly into pan. Mix filling ingredients. Pour into pan. Bake at 425°F for 15 minutes; reduce heat to 350°F and bake for 55 minutes longer.

**What the mother sings to the cradle goes all
the way down to the coffin.**
Henry Ward Beecher

FLAPPER PIE

Janette Oke
a Favorite

■ ■ ■ ■ ■ ■ ■ ■ ■ ■ ■

INGREDIENTS

7 double graham wafers
  (rolled fine)
1/2 cup sugar
1/4 cup butter (melted)
1/2 teaspoon ground cinnamon

FILLING
2 cups milk
2 egg yolks
2 tablespoons cornstarch
1/4 cup sugar
1 teaspoon vanilla (or fruit)

PREPARATION

Mix together wafers, 1/2 cup sugar, butter, and cinnamon; remove 1/2 cup of mixture for top of pie. Use remaining mixture to line the bottom of the pie tin. Add cooked filling. Beat the egg whites to make a meringue. Spread over top and sprinkle remaining crumb mixture. Note: A lemon filling is good, too!

I AM blessed with a husband who has been patient with me as a "practicing" young bride, a harassed busy mother, and an I-don't-want-to-spend-all-of-my-time-in-the-kitchen grandmother.

Edward has always been easy to cook for and appreciative of the effort that goes into the meal. But he does have favorites. One of them is butter tarts. I don't make them often any more (neither of us needs the calories), but I can be sure that they will be enjoyed—and viewed as a special little love offering just for him.

BUTTER TARTS

Aunt Joyce Deal

INGREDIENTS

4 cups raisins

$2^2/_3$ cups butter

8 cups brown sugar

1 can evaporated milk

8 eggs (beaten)

4 teaspoons vanilla

PREPARATION

Soak raisins in boiling water for 5 minutes. Pour off water. Add butter and sugar to raisins. Blend until butter melts. Add milk and eggs. Add vanilla. Pour into prepared unbaked tart shells. Bake at 400°F until top is golden brown.

MINCEMEAT

Great Grandma Violet Ruggles

■ ■ ■ ■ ■ ■ ■ ■ ■ ■ ■

INGREDIENTS

2 cups chopped cooked beef

4 cups apples

2 cups raisins

2 teaspoons salt

1 cup suet

2 cups sugar

1 cup apple cider or vinegar

1 tablespoon cinnamon

1 tablespoon nutmeg

1 teaspoon cloves

1 cup meat stock

juice of $1/2$ lemon

PREPARATION

Cook slowly in pot on stove until thick. Stir often.

Cousins Katie & Courtney: Still can't figure 'em out!

17

Quick Breads

COFFEE CAKE

Great Aunt Leone Edenloff

■ ■ ■ ■ ■ ■ ■ ■ ■ ■ ■ ■

INGREDIENTS

MIXTURE

1 cup brown sugar

4 tablespoons melted butter

4 tablespoons flour

4 teaspoons cinnamon

1 cup chopped nuts

BATTER

1 cup shortening

$1^1/_2$ cups sugar

2 eggs

1 cup milk

$3^1/_2$ cups flour

4 teaspoons baking powder

salt

PREPARATION

Spread part of batter in greased, oblong pan. Spread half of mixture over batter. Add rest of batter then top with rest of mixture. Bake for 45 minutes at 350°F.

■ ■ ■ ■ ■ ■ ■ ■ ■ ■ ■ ■

**I do like a little bit
of butter to my bread.**

A. A. Milne

CHEDDAR APPLE MUFFINS
Barbara Oke

INGREDIENTS

3 cups all-purpose flour
$2/3$ cup sugar
4 teaspoons baking powder
1 teaspoon salt
1 teaspoon ground cinnamon
2 eggs

$1^1/_2$ cups shredded cheddar
  cheese
1 cup apple juice
$^1/_2$ cup butter (melted)
2 cups finely chopped apple
  (pared)

PREPARATION

In large bowl, combine flour, sugar, baking powder, salt, and cinnamon. Add cheese; mix. Beat eggs with apple juice; stir in butter and apple. Add all at once to flour mixture; stir until moistened. Divide batter among 12 large greased muffin cups. Bake in 375°F oven for 25 to 30 minutes. Makes 1 dozen muffins.

**Good family life is never an accident but
always an achievement by those who share it.**
James H. S. Bossard

DATE MUFFINS

Grandma Amy Steeves

∎ ∎ ∎ ∎ ∎ ∎ ∎ ∎ ∎ ∎ ∎

INGREDIENTS

1/4 cup butter	1/3 cup sugar
1 egg	1/2 teaspoon salt
1 cup milk	1 teaspoon baking soda
1 cup bran (natural bran)	1 teaspoon baking powder
1 cup flour	1/2 to 1 cup dates or raisins

PREPARATION

Combine ingredients, bake at 350°F for 15 to 20 minutes.

Courtney & Ashley baking muffins at Grandmother Janette's

BRAN MUFFINS
Aunt Marge Wiens

■ ■ ■ ■ ■ ■ ■ ■ ■ ■ ■ ■

INGREDIENTS

2 cups natural bran
2 cup boiling water
1 cup raisins
1 cup shortening
3 cups sugar
4 eggs

1 quart sour milk
5 cups flour
3 teaspoons baking soda
1 teaspoon salt
4 cups bran flakes

PREPARATION

Mix natural bran, boiling water, and raisins; set aside. Cream shortening, sugar, and eggs. Add sour milk. In another bowl mix flour, soda, and salt. Add wet ingredients to dry. Fold in 4 cups bran flakes. Bake at 350°F for 15 to 20 minutes. Batter will keep several weeks in refrigerator. Note: Can use 4 cups bran and 3 cups boiling water with no bran flakes. Makes 36 muffins.

■ ■ ■ ■ ■ ■ ■ ■ ■ ■ ■ ■

**Doing little things with a strong desire to
please God makes them really great.**
St. Francis De Sales

DONUTS

Aunt Joyce Deal

■ ■ ■ ■ ■ ■ ■ ■ ■ ■ ■ ■

INGREDIENTS

2 tablespoons shortening
1 cup sugar
2 eggs (beaten)
1 cup milk
1 teaspoon vanilla

1 cup flour
3 teaspoons baking powder
$1/2$ teaspoon salt
$1/8$ teaspoon nutmeg

PREPARATION

Cream shortening and sugar. Add eggs, milk, and vanilla. Combine flour, baking powder, salt, and nutmeg; mix with wet ingredients. Add enough additional flour to make soft, workable dough. Roll out dough to $1/2$-inch thickness and cut. Drop into hot oil to deep fry. Sugar while warm (kids love holes). Can be frozen. Reheat in oven or microwave for fresh donut taste.

DONUT making was a family affair. All our kids were interested in what was going on in the kitchen. When they were small, Saturday was my baking day, and I soon learned to have them take turns so I wouldn't have four little people fighting over who got to stir. But donut day was different. We made an assembly line. One child stirred the ingredients. One rolled and cut the dough. I did the frying. Another dipped the donuts into the sugar and another stacked them in the pan to cool. They shifted tasks frequently, and when we were done they had milk and fresh donuts while I cleaned up the mess.

SKY-HIGH BISCUITS

Janette Oke

■ ■ ■ ■ ■ ■ ■ ■ ■ ■ ■ ■

INGREDIENTS

2 cups flour (white)

1 cup whole wheat flour

$4^{1}/_{2}$ teaspoons baking powder

2 tablespoons sugar

$^{1}/_{2}$ teaspoon salt

$^{3}/_{4}$ teaspoon cream of tartar

$^{3}/_{4}$ cup butter or margarine

1 egg (beaten)

1 cup milk

PREPARATION

Combine flour, baking powder, sugar, salt, and tartar. Cut in butter; add egg and milk. Roll out dough and pat to 1-inch thickness. Cut and bake at 450°F for 12 to 15 minutes.

CHEESE BISCUITS

Janette Oke

■ ■ ■ ■ ■ ■ ■ ■ ■ ■ ■ ■

INGREDIENTS

2 cups all-purpose flour

1 tablespoon baking powder

1 teaspoon salt

$^1/_4$ cup butter or margarine

$^1/_2$ cup shredded cheddar cheese

$^3/_4$ cup milk

PREPARATION

Preheat oven to 450°F. In large bowl, mix flour, baking powder, and salt. With pastry blender cut in cheese and butter until mixture resembles coarse crumbs. Stir in milk with fork just until mixture forms a soft dough that leaves the side of bowl. Turn dough onto lightly floured surface; knead six to eight times to mix thoroughly. Do not knead for too long or dough will get tough. Roll out dough to $^1/_2$-inch thickness with floured rolling pin, rolling lightly as you near the edges to keep dough an even thickness. Cut into biscuits with floured $2^1/_2$-inch round cutter. Place biscuits on ungreased cookie sheet. Press dough trimmings together. Reroll and cut more biscuits. Bake 12 to 15 minutes until biscuits are golden brown. Makes about 12 biscuits.

CRANBERRY BREAD

Beth Wiens

INGREDIENTS

2 cups flour

1 cup sugar

$1/2$ teaspoon salt

$1/2$ teaspoon baking soda

$11/2$ teaspoon baking powder

1 egg

2 tablespoons oil

2 tablespoons hot water

$1/2$ cup orange juice

$11/2$ cups cranberries

$1/2$ cup chopped nuts

PREPARATION

Mix flour, sugar, salt, soda, and baking powder. Add egg, oil, hot water, orange juice, cranberries, and chopped nuts. Bake at 325°F for 1 hour.

We need love's tender lessons taught
As only weakness can;
God hath his small interpreters;
The child must teach the man.

John Greenleaf Whittier

SUGARLESS LOAF
Great Grandma Violet Ruggles

■ ■ ■ ■ ■ ■ ■ ■ ■ ■ ■ ■

INGREDIENTS

1 cup raisins
1 cup dates
1 orange
2 cups flour
1 teaspoon baking soda
$1/2$ teaspoon nutmeg
$1/2$ teaspoon salt
1 egg

1 cup milk
2 tablespoons shortening
1 teaspoon vanilla

PREPARATION

Put raisins, dates, and orange through food processor. Add flour and other dry ingredients. Mix with fingertips. Beat egg and milk. Add melted shortening and vanilla; mix. Pour into large, greased loaf tin and bake at 350°F for 1 hour.

Great Grandma Violet Ruggles was the mother of ten children, including twin girls. She is pictured here with Lorne & Lavon, her twin great-grandsons.

GRANDMA'S HOTCAKES

Debbie Oke

■ ■ ■ ■ ■ ■ ■ ■ ■ ■ ■

INGREDIENTS

2 cups buttermilk

2 teaspoons baking soda

$3/_4$ teaspoon salt

$1/_2$ cup sour cream

2 eggs

1 cup flour

$2/_3$ cup sugar

$3/_4$ teaspoon baking powder

$1/_2$ cup oats (uncooked)

$1/_4$ teaspoon yellow cornmeal

PREPARATION

Put buttermilk, soda, and salt in mixing bowl. Add sour cream; stir until mixture foams. Add eggs, beating with spoon. Mix flour, sugar, baking powder, oatmeal, and cornmeal; add to liquid ingredients. Beat until smooth. Pour batter on hot greased griddle.

Kristie: Where's the syrup?

BUTTERMILK WAFFLES

Debbie Oke

INGREDIENTS

2 cups flour

1/4 teaspoon baking soda

1 1/2 teaspoons baking powder

1 tablespoon sugar

1/2 teaspoon salt

2 eggs (separated)

1 3/4 cups buttermilk

6 tablespoons butter (melted)

PREPARATION

In large mixing bowl, combine dry ingredients. In medium bowl, beat egg yolks until light. Add buttermilk and butter. Combine liquid ingredients with dry ingredients with a few quick strokes. In small bowl, beat egg whites until stiff but not dry. Fold into batter and bake in waffle iron. Makes 3 10-inch waffles.

Cousins Alex & Kristie

18
...
Relishes, etc.

PICCADILLI

Barbara Oke

■ ■ ■ ■ ■ ■ ■ ■ ■ ■ ■ ■

INGREDIENTS

1 quart green tomatoes
2 medium sweet red peppers
2 medium sweet green peppers
2 large mild onions
1 small head cabbage
$^1/_2$ cup salt

3 cups vinegar
2 cups brown sugar
(firmly packed)
1 teaspoon mustard
2 teaspoons pickling salt

PREPARATION

Chop vegetables. Combine and cover with salt. Let stand overnight. Drain and press; add remaining ingredients. Simmer until clear. Fill jars till full. Seal tightly.

Cousins Courtney & Katie

CHOW CHOW

Great Grandma Violet Ruggles

INGREDIENTS

1 bowl cabbage

1 bowl green tomatoes

$1/2$ bowl onions (chopped)

1 cup vinegar

1 cup sugar

1 cup water

spices

PREPARATION

Salt cabbage, tomatoes, and onions and let stand overnight. Drain and boil for a few minutes in vinegar, sugar, water, and spices. Pour into prepared jars. Seal.

Katie:
Sometimes pretend
food is better

1000 ISLAND PICKLES

Grandma Amy Steeves

■ ■ ■ ■ ■ ■ ■ ■ ■ ■ ■ ■

INGREDIENTS

8 large cucumbers
1 large cauliflower
12 onions
2 red peppers
2 green peppers
$1/_2$ cup salt
8 cups vinegar

6 cups sugar
1 tablespoon mustard seed
1 tablespoon celery
$3/_4$ cup flour
6 teaspoons mustard
1 tablespoon turmeric

PREPARATION

Wipe the cucumbers but do not peel. Break cauliflower apart.
Peel onions. Remove seeds and membranes from peppers. Put
all through the food chopper. Sprinkle with salt. Add 5 cups
water. Let stand 1 hour and then drain. Boil remaining ingredients
for 20 minutes.

■ ■ ■ ■ ■ ■ ■ ■ ■ ■ ■ ■

**Character, good or bad, has a tendency
to perpetrate itself.**
A. A. Hodge

BREAD AND BUTTER PICKLES
Grandma Amy Steever

■ ■ ■ ■ ■ ■ ■ ■ ■ ■ ■ ■

INGREDIENTS

6 quarts sliced green cucumbers
12 sliced onions
1 teaspoon alum
8 cups vinegar
$1/4$ cup mustard seed

2 tablespoons tumeric
1 tablespoon whole cloves
2 teaspoons celery seed
6 cups sugar

PREPARATION

Slice cucumbers; sprinkle with $1/2$ cup pickling salt. Cover with boiling water and let cool 3 hours. Add alum; drain. Boil vinegar, mustard seed, turmeric, cloves, celery seed, and sugar. Add cucumbers and onions. Boil 20 to 30 minutes. Bottle and seal. Makes 6 quarts.

■ ■ ■ ■ ■ ■ ■ ■ ■ ■ ■ ■

**Character is much easier kept
than recovered.**
Thomas Paine

CORN RELISH

Great Grandma Violet Ruggles

■ ■ ■ ■ ■ ■ ■ ■ ■ ■ ■ ■

INGREDIENTS

18 ears corn

1 small cabbage (shredded)

3 green peppers (diced)

1/4 cup salt

4 good sized onions (diced)

3 cups sugar

3 tablespoons ground mustard

2 cups vinegar

PREPARATION

Cut corn off the cob. Combine all ingredients in large pot. Bring to simmer and cook for 15 minutes. Pour into jars and seal.

■ ■ ■ ■ ■ ■ ■ ■ ■ ■ ■ ■

No man may choose
what coming hours may bring
To him in need, of joy, or suffering.
But what his soul shall
bring unto each hour
To meet the challenge—
this is his power.

Priscilla Leonard

19
...
Salads & Dressings

ITALIAN BROCCOLI/ CAULIFLOWER SALAD

Debbie Oke

INGREDIENTS

1 pound broccoli (washed and cut in florets)

1 pound cauliflower (washed and cut in florets)

2 cans or jars button mushrooms

1/2 purple onion (sliced)

1 to 2 carrots (sliced)

DRESSING

1 1/4 cups oil

1 package Good Seasoning Italian dressing

1/4 cup vinegar

1 1/2 tablespoons sugar

PREPARATION

Blend dressing in blender. Pour over salad 10 minutes before serving.

**Eat breakfast like a king;
eat lunch like a prince;
but eat dinner like a pauper.**

O. F. Gober

MANDARIN ALMOND SALAD

Debbie Oke

INGREDIENTS

1 head iceberg lettuce (torn into bite-size pieces)

1 head romaine lettuce (torn into bite-size pieces)

2 cups celery (chopped)

6 green onions (chopped)

1 pound mushrooms (sliced)

16-ounce can mandarin oranges

2-ounce package almonds (sliced)

3-ounce package cream cheese (slivered in small pieces)

DRESSING

$1/4$ cup vinegar

$1/4$ cup sugar

$1/2$ cup oil

1 teaspoon salt

2 teaspoons parsley

dash tabasco sauce

PREPARATION

Combine salad in large bowl. Add dressing right before serving.

**Children are God's apostles, day by day
Sent forth to preach of love,
and hope, and peace.**

James Russell Lowell

GRAPEFRUIT-GARLIC DRESSING

Janette Oke

INGREDIENTS

1 cup salad or olive oil

1/2 cup reconstituted frozen
grapefruit juice

1 large clove garlic (crushed)

2 tablespoons chili sauce (or
ketchup)

1 teaspoon salt

1 teaspoon sugar

PREPARATION

Combine all ingredients and shake well. Makes about 1³/₄ cups
dressing.

WHITE CAP YOGURT DRESSING

Janette Oke

INGREDIENTS

1¹/₄ cups plain yogurt

2 tablespoons lemon juice

1/2 teaspoon marjoram

1/2 teaspoon salt

1/4 teaspoon thyme leaves

1/4 teaspoon dill weed

1/4 teaspoon pepper

1 small garlic clove (minced)

PREPARATION

Mix all ingredients. Makes about $1^1/_2$ cups.

TACO SALAD DRESSING

Aunt Joyce Deal

■ ■ ■ ■ ■ ■ ■ ■ ■ ■ ■

INGREDIENTS

$1/_2$ cup vinegar

$1/_2$ cup oil

$1/_2$ teaspoon paprika

$1^1/_2$ teaspoons prepared mustard

1 cup sugar

$1/_2$ teaspoon Worcestershire sauce

$1/_2$ teaspoon salt

1 cup ketchup

$1^1/_4$ cup Miracle Whip

$1/_2$ teaspoon pepper

PREPARATION

Mix in order given. Blend well.

■ ■ ■ ■ ■ ■ ■ ■ ■ ■ ■

**Lettuce, like conversation, requires a good
deal of oil, to avoid friction, and keep
the company smooth.**

Charles Dudley Warner

PARMESAN LAYER SALAD

Janette Oke
Lavon's Favorite

■ ■ ■ ■ ■ ■ ■ ■ ■ ■ ■ ■

INGREDIENTS

1 head lettuce (torn)

1 cup celery (diced)

4 hard boiled eggs (sliced)

10-ounce package frozen peas
  (uncooked)

$1/_2$ cup green peppers (optional)

1 medium onion (diced)

8 slices bacon (fried and diced)

2 cups real mayonnaise

$1/_4$ cup sugar

$1/_3$ cup parmesan cheese

4 ounces cheddar cheese
  (grated)

PREPARATION

In a large bowl or deep dish layer the lettuce, celery, eggs, frozen peas, peppers, onion, and bacon in order. Mix the mayonnaise, sugar, and parmesan cheese; spread over salad. Top with grated cheese. Cover and refrigerate for 8 to 12 hours.

■ ■ ■ ■ ■ ■ ■ ■ ■ ■ ■ ■

**Condiments are like old friends—
highly thought of, but often taken for granted.**
Marilyn Kaytor

SOUR CREAM SALAD DRESSING

Great Grandma Violet Ruggles

■ ■ ■ ■ ■ ■ ■ ■ ■ ■ ■ ■

INGREDIENTS

1 cup vinegar

1 cup sugar

1 teaspoon salt

1 dessert spoon (teaspoon)
  dry mustard (heaping)

1 tablespoon cornstarch

1 teaspoon salt

2 eggs

1 cup sour cream

1 dessert spoon butter

PREPARATION

Boil vinegar (may dilute vinegar with $^1/_4$ cup water). Mix dry ingredients and add eggs. Beat well. Add sour cream and stir into hot vinegar. Add butter last. This dressing can be diluted with cream when using. (She always mixed the mustard with the sugar.)

*Cousins Nate & Ashley
ready for a ride*

JACKIE'S FANTASTIC FRENCH DRESSING

Barbara Oke

INGREDIENTS

1/4 cup lemon juice
1/4 cup vinegar
3/4 cup salad oil
1/2 teaspoon salt
1/4 teaspoon pepper

1/4 teaspoon dry mustard
1/4 teaspoon paprika
1/4 teaspoon sugar
1/8 teaspoon garlic powder

PREPARATION

Measure all ingredients into a jar with a tight-fitting lid. Put the lid on the jar and shake vigorously. Yields about 2 1/2 cups of French Dressing. Note: Always shake before serving.

Children can have no better inheritance than believing parents. Religion can become real in the midst of the family as in practically no other way. Many of us have inherited great riches from our parents—the bank account of their personal faith and family prayers.

Nels F. S. Ferre

20
...
Tips

KITCHEN HELPS

■ ■ ■ ■ ■ ■ ■ ■ ■ ■ ■ ■

1. To keep fruit from darkening (e.g., bananas, apples, and pears) dip them in lemon or pineapple juice.

2. A leaf of lettuce dropped into soup will help absorb the fat. Remove leaf before serving.

3. Store leftover vegetables in a resealable bag to use later in soup.

4. Freeze soup stock in freezer trays, then in a bag. Use in recipes that call for small amounts.

5. Use kitchen shears to chop canned tomatoes in the can.

6. Remove the last few silks that cling to corn kernels by rubbing with a moist paper towel.

7. Cover a peach with boiling water and allow to stand for a few seconds. Peel will come off easily. (This works with tomatoes as well.)

8. Use a vegetable peeler to make chocolate curls.

9. Rub lemon on fishy smelling hands.

10. To soften or keep softness in brown sugar, place half an apple in the container and close tightly.

11. Place a couple of salted crackers in granulated sugar container to keep from lumping.

12. To relieve dry, chapped hands:
    a. mix 1 teaspoon of white sugar and 1 teaspoon of petroleum jelly

b. rub hands for several minutes

c. wash hands using plenty of gentle soap and warm water

d. apply moisturizing lotion

13. Muffins bake best in humid air. Put water in any unused cups of a muffin pan.

14. To keep the yolks from crumbling when slicing hard cooked eggs, wet the knife before each cut.

15. Place bay leaves in a tea bag or cheesecloth for easy removal from stews or sauces.

16. For a rich, brown crust, rub mayonnaise generously over skin of roasted chicken before cooking.

17. Partially frozen meat will slice easily.

18. Tomatoes will ripen over-night if stored in a brown paper bag in a dark pantry.

19. Use greased muffin tins as molds for baking stuffed peppers or for baking mini-meat loaves.

20. Tenderize meat by rubbing both sides with vinegar and olive oil. Allow to stand 2 hours before cooking.

21. Substitute mayonnaise for shortening or oil for added moisture and tender tex-ture.

22. Put flour in a large salt shaker for use when flour-ing cake pans. It's efficient and less messy.

23. Use an egg slicer to slice stemmed mushrooms.

24. Use unwaxed dental floss to split cake layers.

25. Use an ice cream scoop to fill muffin pans.

TIME-SAVERS

■ ■ ■ ■ ■ ■ ■ ■ ■ ■ ■

1. Bake or boil enough unpeeled potatoes for a week. Refrigerate in plastic bags for future use.
2. Brown several servings of ground beef, turkey, or chicken at once. Freeze in 1-pound containers or bags for later use.
3. Kitchen scissors cut pizza fast and don't scratch the pan.
4. Melt chocolate or chocolate chips in microwave on medium for 2 to 4 minutes, stirring every minute.
5. Brown a whole pound of bacon; cool and crumble. Store in freezer and use a little at a time when needed for a recipe.
6. Use a pizza cutter to cut bars and sandwiches into strips or squares in a fraction of the time.

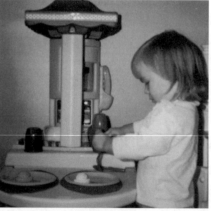

Katie tries out new "timesaving" bake center.

MICROWAVE

■ ■ ■ ■ ■ ■ ■ ■ ■ ■ ■ ■

1. Soften 1 quart of ice cream on defrost for 30 to 40 seconds.

2. Soften cream cheese by heating on high for 15 seconds. Wrap in plastic wrap.

3. To peel tomatoes easily, heat on high for 15 seconds. Let stand for 1 minute before peeling.

4. To soften hardened brown sugar, place opened package in microwave with 1 cup hot water. Microwave side by side on high for $1^1/_2$ to 2 minutes for a half pound, or 2 to 3 minutes for 1 pound.

5. One stick of butter or margarine will soften in 1 minute when microwaved at 20% power.

6. Soften one 8-ounce package of cream cheese by microwaving at 30% power for 2 to $2^1/_2$ minutes. One 3-ounce package of cream cheese will soften in $1^1/_2$ to 2 minutes.

7. To scald milk, cook 1 cup for 2 to $2^1/_2$ minutes, stirring once each minute.

8. To make dry bread crumbs, cut six slices of bread into $1/_2$-inch cubes. Microwave in 3-quart casserole 6 to 7 minutes, or until dry, stirring after 3 minutes. Crush in blender.

9. Refresh stale potato chips, crackers, or other similar snacks by putting a plateful in the microwave oven for 30 to 45 seconds. Let stand

for 1 minute to crisp. Cereals can also be crisped.

10. Melt marshmallow creme in the microwave oven.

Half of a 7-ounce jar will melt in 35 to 40 seconds on high. Stir to blend.

MANY of the old recipes seemed to assume that a woman knew her way around the kitchen. Many of them simply listed the ingredients and gave no instruction as to what to do with them. When Mom taught us to cook she used vocal instructions such as "a lump of butter" or "a scant cup of sugar" or "a pinch of this" or "dab of that." That was how we learned to cook. Many of Mom's recipes were not even written down. We made-do with whatever was in the cupboard, improvising and adjusting as necessary. Substitutes were common. Basic recipes were memorized. We did not spend much time flipping through recipe books before deciding what to have for dinner.

SUBSTITUTES

■ ■ ■ ■ ■ ■ ■ ■ ■ ■ ■ ■

1. **Low-calorie butter**
   (7 calories per tablespoon)
   1 pint lowfat cottage cheese
   4 tablespoons powdered
      milk
   $1/4$ cup water
   2 packages butter buds
   2 packages sugar substitute
   1 drop yellow food coloring
   Whip in blender until
   smooth. Refrigerate.

2. **Egg**
   $1/4$ cup skim milk
   1 teaspoon vegetable oil
   1 teaspoon nonfat dry milk
      powder
   3 egg whites

   Beat first three ingredients.
   With a fork, beat lightly 3
   egg whites into other ingredients. Makes two eggs and
   may be frozen.

3. **Sweetened condensed milk**
   $1/4$ cup margarine
   1 cup boiling water
   2 cups sugar
   4 cups skim milk powder
   In medium bowl dissolve
   margarine in boiling water.
   Add sugar. Beat with beater
   until dissolved. Gradually
   add skim milk powder.
   Makes 1 quart. Will keep
   in refrigerator up to a year.

CLEANING

1. Cleaning solution:
   1 cup ammonia
   $^1/_2$ cup vinegar
   $^1/_4$ cup soda
   1 gallon warm water
2. Club soda cleans and shines kitchen appliances.
3. For a grease-clogged sink, pour in 1 cup salt and 1 cup baking soda. Then pour in 1 kettle of boiling water.
4. Toilet bowl cleaner will help remove water ring from glass on crystal vases. Dampen first with water, then with the cleaners. Allow to sit.

5. Use Worcestershire sauce to clean and shine copper pots.
6. Spray barbeque grills and broiler pan with non-stick cooking spray for easier clean-up.
7. Line bottom of grill with heavy-duty aluminum foil for easy clean up of ashes.
8. To clean a blender, put a little soapy water in it, place the cover on it, and turn it on.
9. A toothbrush is handy for cleaning beaters, graters, and similar kitchen utensils.

21
...
Unexpected Guests

FRUIT DIP

Debbie Oke

■ ■ ■ ■ ■ ■ ■ ■ ■ ■ ■ ■

INGREDIENTS

8-ounce package strawberry
  cream cheese
8 ounces marshmallow creme
fruit slices of apple, pear,

orange, kiwi, strawberries, and
  bananas (cut in fourths with
  peel left on)
pineapple juice

PREPARATION

Combine cream cheese and marshmallow creme until smooth.
Cut fruit. Dip ends of bananas, apple, and pear slices in pineapple juice (to prevent darkening).

*Kristie: I say just feed them
oatmeal. It's good enough for me;
why isn't it good enough for
company?*

CHILI DIP

Debbie Oke

■ ■ ■ ■ ■ ■ ■ ■ ■ ■ ■ ■

INGREDIENTS

1 can chili (with or without
  beans)

$^1/_2$ cup cheddar cheese (grated)

8-ounce package cream cheese
  (softened)

PREPARATION

Mix chili and cream cheese until smooth. Bake at 350°F for 30 minutes, or in microwave until bubbly. Sprinkle cheddar cheese on top. Serve with tortilla chips.

■ ■ ■ ■ ■ ■ ■ ■ ■ ■ ■

Children are the true connoisseurs.
What's precious to them has
no price—only value.
Bel Kaufman

SEVEN-LAYER CASSEROLE

Debbie Oke

■ ■ ■ ■ ■ ■ ■ ■ ■ ■ ■

INGREDIENTS

$1/2$ cup uncooked rice

1 can corn (undrained)

$1/2$ cup bell pepper (chopped, optional)

1 small can tomato sauce

1 lb ground beef or turkey

(cooked and drained)

1 can tomato sauce

1 can water

4 strips bacon (cut in 1 inch pieces)

$1/2$ cup onion (chopped)

PREPARATION

Layer in order given in 9 x 13-inch pan. Bake at 350°F for 1 hour covered and $1/2$ hour uncovered.

■ ■ ■ ■ ■ ■ ■ ■ ■ ■ ■

Children have never been very good at listening to their elders, but they have never failed to imitate them.

James Baldwin

TUNA-CHOW MEIN CASSEROLE

Debbie Oke

INGREDIENTS

3-ounce can chow mein noodles

1 can tuna

1 can mushroom soup

$1/3$ cup milk

1 small can mushrooms

$3/4$ cup celery (finely diced)

$1/4$ cup onion (minced)

$1/3$ cup cashews (or other nuts)

dash of salt or pepper

PREPARATION

Mix all ingredients except $1/2$ cup of noodles. Sprinkle noodles on top. Bake at 325°F for 40 minutes. May use chicken or cream of chicken soup.

That energy which makes a child hard to manage is the energy which afterward makes him a manager of life.

Henry Ward Beecher

SQUARES

Grandma Amy Steeves

■ ■ ■ ■ ■ ■ ■ ■ ■ ■ ■ ■

INGREDIENTS

24 finely crushed graham wafers

1 tin sweetened milk

2 cups miniature marshmallows

1 cup chopped nuts

2 cups red and green glazed cherries

PREPARATION

Mix and form in pan. Cut in squares.

Alex learns to share with cousin Kristie at his first birthday party.

UNCOOKED COOKIES

Great-great Aunt Myrtle Steeves

■ ■ ■ ■ ■ ■ ■ ■ ■ ■ ■ ■

INGREDIENTS

34 graham crackers

34 colored marshmallows

$^1/_2$ cup nuts

1 can Eagle Brand sweetened
    condensed milk

PREPARATION

Mix together. Roll and chill. Slice and serve.

Jackie making cookies at Grandma Janette's

WACKY CAKE

Grandma Amy Steeves

■ ■ ■ ■ ■ ■ ■ ■ ■ ■ ■

INGREDIENTS

20-ounce tin crushed pineapple
  and juice

20-ounce tin cherry pie filling

1 large golden cake mix

$1^1/_3$ cups flaked coconut

1 cup melted butter

PREPARATION

In a 9 x 13-inch pan, spread ingredients in layers. Drizzle butter
over layers. Bake in 350°F oven for 1 hour.

Cousins Alex & Kristie

22

Vegetables

CREAMY NEW POTATOES AND PEAS

Grandma Amy Steeves

■ ■ ■ ■ ■ ■ ■ ■ ■ ■ ■ ■ ■

INGREDIENTS

small new potatoes | fresh peas

PREPARATION

Boil potatoes in salted water. Boil peas in water with 1 tablespoon sugar and salt. When potatoes are cooked (but not mushy), lift them into pea kettle. Drain excess water. Add cream. Boil for short time. Salt and pepper to taste. Watch closely.

MOM'S birthday is July 30th. She always tried to celebrate with fresh new potatoes and peas. In Alberta it is not always possible to have potatoes of eating size by that date—but usually we made it. Mom cooked the tender new potatoes, then added the crisp new peas to the pot. She covered this with sweet farm milk, heavy with cream and seasoned to taste. Delicious!

Mom is in an Extended Care facility now, and last year for her birthday my Uncle Burt paid his visit with a dish of her

PARSNIPS AND CARROTS

Janette Oke

■ ■ ■ ■ ■ ■ ■ ■ ■ ■ ■ ■

INGREDIENTS

parsnips and carrots

butter

seasoning

PREPARATION

Cut washed and peeled vegetables into finger lengths. Boil or steam until tender. (Note: parsnips will not need as much cooking time as carrots. Do not overcook.) Place in frying pan with small amount of butter. Heat and turn. Season lightly. Sprinkle with chopped parsley.

much-loved creamed peas and potatoes. Since Aunt Carrie has been gone now for several years, Uncle Burt has become a great cook. Mom enjoyed the tasty dish more than ever because it was made with an extra ingredient: Love!

Grandma Amy Steeves

SWEET AND SOUR GREEN BEANS
Debbie Oke

■ ■ ■ ■ ■ ■ ■ ■ ■ ■ ■ ■

INGREDIENTS

2 teaspoons prepared mustard
  (from jar)
2 tablespoons sugar
$1/2$ cup butter

$1/2$ teaspoon salt
2 tablespoons vinegar
3 cups hot, cooked green beans

PREPARATION

Combine mustard, sugar, butter, and salt. Heat slowly, stirring constantly. Stir in vinegar. Pour over green beans. Heat thoroughly.

■ ■ ■ ■ ■ ■ ■ ■ ■ ■ ■ ■

**It is true that a child is always hungry
all over; but he is also curious all over,
and his curiosity is excited about
as early as his hunger.**
Charles Dudley Warner

VEGETABLE SURPRISE
Debbie Oke

INGREDIENTS

1 stick margarine

3 cups Rice Krispies

2 10-ounce packages frozen
  mixed vegetables

1 can mushroom soup

1 package dry onion soup mix

1 cup sour cream

1 can sliced water chestnuts

PREPARATION

Melt margarine and brown Rice Krispies. Mix remaining ingredients in large casserole and top with Rice Krispies. Bake at 350°F for 1 hour.

LAUREL'S Nate was not very old when his daddy, Marvin, had to make a business trip out of town.

"Now, Nate," he said as he told him goodbye, "while I'm gone you'll be the man of the house."

"Oh, no," groaned the little boy, "now I'll have to eat peas."

CHEDDAR TOMATO CASSEROLE
Barbara Oke

■ ■ ■ ■ ■ ■ ■ ■ ■ ■ ■ ■

INGREDIENTS

8 slices bacon (chopped)
1/4 cup sliced green onions
3/4 cup diced tomatoes
1 tablespoon flour
1/2 teaspoon salt
6 eggs

1 cup milk
1 1/4 cups shredded cheddar
  cheese
1 tablespoon grated parmesan
  cheese

PREPARATION

Cook bacon until crisp; reserve 1 tablespoon drippings. Saute onions in reserved drippings until tender; add tomatoes to pan. Sprinkle flour and salt over vegetables; toss lightly. Beat together eggs and milk; add vegetable mixture. Add 1 cup cheddar cheese and cooked bacon. Pour into greased, 2-quart baking dish. Sprinkle with parmesan cheese. Bake in 350°F oven for 25 to 30 minutes. Remove from oven. Sprinkle with remaining cheddar cheese and let stand for 5 minutes. Makes 4 servings.

23

Wet Your Whistle

LOVE PUNCH

Janette Oke

■ ■ ■ ■ ■ ■ ■ ■ ■ ■ ■ ■ ■

INGREDIENTS

2 10-ounce packages frozen sliced strawberries (slightly thawed)

2 6-ounce cans frozen orange juice concentrate

1 quart ginger ale

PREPARATION

Puree strawberries in blender. Add undiluted orange concentrate. Mix thoroughly. Divide among six or eight glasses. Fill to the top with ginger ale.

GRANDDAUGHTER Ashley had her first tea party when she was still in a high-chair. Great-grandmother Mabelle Oke and I were her guests. From then on she was a fan of the occasion. The first thing she would ask for when she came to my house was a tea party. The tea was mostly milk, but she was allowed to pour and that was the fun of it. She also loved to stir. She would pour and sip and stir and sip. The party could go on and on. She didn't have to worry about her tea getting cold; it wasn't hot to start with. Little by little she added things to her tea parties. I was to call her

PINK PARTY SLUSH

Janette Oke

■ ■ ■ ■ ■ ■ ■ ■ ■ ■ ■ ■

INGREDIENTS

1 gallon cranberry juice cocktail
1 quart 7-Up or ginger ale

46-ounce can pineapple-
grapefruit drink

PREPARATION

Combine ingredients just before serving. Makes 1¹/₂ gallons or
50 servings. To dress up punch, float thin slices of orange and
lemon in punch. Serve over ice.

Ashley's first tea party

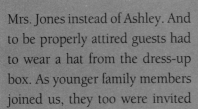

Mrs. Jones instead of Ashley. And
to be properly attired guests had
to wear a hat from the dress-up
box. As younger family members
joined us, they too were invited
to the tea parties. But so far, none of them has developed
the same understanding of the occasion as Ashley. They
gulp and devour and rush off to play. Oh, they enjoy it,
but no one else has been able to stretch a tea party into a
whole afternoon of enjoyment as Ashley does.

MOCHA INTERNATIONAL COFFEE MIX

Debbie Oke

INGREDIENTS

2 cups powdered non-dairy
  creamer
1 1/3 cups nonfat dry milk
1/3 cup cocoa
1 3/4 cups sugar

1 cup instant coffee
1/2 teaspoon cinnamon
  (optional)
1/2 teaspoon nutmeg (optional)

PREPARATION

Blend ingredients in blender on high for 2 minutes. Mix 2 to 3 teaspoons into 1 cup of boiling water.

"Mrs. Jones" entertains teddy at Grandma Janette's.

HOT CRANBERRY CIDER
Debbie Oke

■ ■ ■ ■ ■ ■ ■ ■ ■ ■ ■ ■

INGREDIENTS

$1/2$ gallon apple cider

32 ounces cranberry juice cocktail

$1/2$ cup lemon juice

$1/3$ cup packed brown sugar

8 whole cloves

2 cinnamon sticks

PREPARATION

Heat ingredients in large pan to boiling. Reduce and simmer uncovered for 10 minutes. Remove spices and serve warm.

"Mrs. Jones" takes tea alone at Grandma Janette's.

SUNSHINE PUNCH

Barbara Oke

■ ■ ■ ■ ■ ■ ■ ■ ■ ■ ■ ■

INGREDIENTS

1 can frozen orange juice
(thawed)

1 can frozen pineapple juice
(thawed)

1 can frozen apple juice
(thawed)

1 bottle ginger ale

ice

lemon slices

PREPARATION

Mix first four ingredients in a punch bowl. Pour in enough water to almost fill bowl. Add ice and float lemon slices on top.

Courtney, Ashley, & friend have tea at Grandmother Janette's.

24

XTRAs

Snacks & Confections

CRAZY CRUNCH

Aunt Marge Wiens

■ ■ ■ ■ ■ ■ ■ ■ ■ ■ ■ ■

INGREDIENTS

2 quarts popcorn (popped)
$1^1/_3$ cups pecans or walnuts
$^2/_3$ cup almonds or filberts
$1^1/_3$ cups sugar

$^1/_2$ cup margarine
$^1/_2$ cup corn syrup
1 teaspoon vanilla

PREPARATION

Mix together popcorn and nuts. Boil sugar, margarine, and corn syrup for 10 to 15 minutes, stirring constantly. Add vanilla. Cook until a hard ball forms when a few drops are added to cold water. Pour over corn and nuts. Mix well. Cool. Break apart and store in tightly covered container.

Jackie helps brother Alex learn to walk.

BEST EVER BRITTLE

Janette Oke

INGREDIENTS

2 cups shelled raw peanuts
1 cup sugar

1 cup white corn syrup
1 tablespoon baking soda

PREPARATION

Butter a baking sheet before you start and keep it handy. Time is precious once you begin. Mix peanuts, sugar, and syrup in a heavy saucepan. Bring to a boil, stirring constantly. Wipe sides of saucepan with a damp pastry brush and cook without stirring to the hardcrack stage (300°F). Remove from heat immediately and quickly stir in soda. It's supposed to foam, so don't worry! Pour mixture immediately onto buttered baking sheet. When cooled enough to touch, stretch to make as thin as possible. When cool, break into pieces. Store in airtight container.

**We find delight in the beauty and happiness
of children that makes the heart
too big for the body.**

Emerson

CHOCO-MALLOW MAPLE FUDGE

Janette Oke

■ ■ ■ ■ ■ ■ ■ ■ ■ ■ ■ ■

INGREDIENTS

1/4 cup margarine

8-ounce package cream cheese (softened)

4 cups icing sugar

4 1-ounce squares unsweetened chocolate (melted)

1 1/2 teaspoons maple flavoring

2 cups miniature marshmallows

PREPARATION

Cream margarine and softened cream cheese until light and fluffy. Gradually add sugar. Stir in chocolate and flavoring, mixing until well blended. Fold in marshmallows. Press into a greased, 8-inch square pan. Chill overnight; cut in squares.

CHOCOLATE PEANUT CLUSTERS

Aunt Joyce Deal

■ ■ ■ ■ ■ ■ ■ ■ ■ ■ ■ ■

INGREDIENTS

8-ounce package semi-sweet chocolate chips

peanuts (or chinese noodles)

2/3 cup Eagle Brand sweetened condensed milk

PREPARATION

Melt chocolate; cool. Add milk; blend. Add peanuts. Drop by spoonfuls onto waxed paper to set.

SUGAR-FROSTED CRUNCHIES

Grandma Amy Steeves

■ ■ ■ ■ ■ ■ ■ ■ ■ ■ ■ ■

INGREDIENTS

6 ounces semi-sweet chocolate | 2 cups sugar-coated flakes

PREPARATION

Melt chocolate pieces and add sugar-coated flakes. Drop by spoonfuls onto greased sheet or waxed paper to set.

WHEN I was a kid we loved a fresh snowfall because it brought with it a wonderful chance for the "ice-cream wagon." As soon as it had snowed sufficiently to make a nice white, fresh pile in some protected spot, we ran out, cup in hand, and scooped up some of the chilly mass.* We then stirred in fresh cream, a bit of sugar, and some vanilla. And presto—instant ice cream. It was so yummy. I can taste it yet. Too bad that my grandchildren have to miss out on it.

I would no longer recommend doing this because of pollution.

TRUFFLES

Janette Oke

■ ■ ■ ■ ■ ■ ■ ■ ■ ■ ■

INGREDIENTS

3 squares semi-sweet chocolate

5 tablespoons unsalted butter

1 egg yolk

$2/3$ cup sifted confectioners
  sugar

1 teaspoon vanilla

COATING
  finely chopped nuts, flaked
  coconut, cocoa, or chocolate
  crumbs

PREPARATION

Melt chocolate in saucepan over very low heat, stirring constantly. Cool. Cream butter with egg yolk. Gradually add sugar, blending well. Stir in chocolate and vanilla. Chill until firm enough to handle. Shape into balls about 1 inch in diameter. Roll in coating. Chill. Store in refrigerator. Makes about 30 candies.

■ ■ ■ ■ ■ ■ ■ ■ ■ ■ ■

There is a little plant called reverence in the corner of my soul's garden, which I love to have watered once a week.

Oliver Wendell Holmes

25
...
Yeast Bread

AUNT ILA'S BREAD

Aunt Ila Steeves

INGREDIENTS

1 cup warm water
2 teaspoons sugar
2 tablespoons yeast
$1/2$ cup hot water
1 cup cold water

1 tablespoon salt
4 tablespoons shortening
$3/4$ cup sugar
8 cups flour

PREPARATION

Combine warm water, 2 teaspoons sugar, and yeast. Let rise 10 minutes. In large bowl melt shortening in hot water. Add remaining water, salt, sugar, and risen yeast. Knead in flour and cover to rise. Let rise until doubled in size. Punch down. Let rise for $1/2$ hour. Make into loaves and put in pans. Bake at 350°F for 50 minutes. Makes 2 loaves.

**Cooking is like love.
It should be entered into with
abandon or not at all.**
Harriet Van Horne

SAVORY SWEET ROLLS
Debbie Oke

■ ■ ■ ■ ■ ■ ■ ■ ■ ■ ■ ■

INGREDIENTS

5 cups all-purpose flour

3 packages yeast

3 cups milk

$2/3$ cup sugar

$3/4$ cup butter or margarine

3 teaspoons salt

6 eggs

6 to 7 cups flour

PREPARATION

Combine 5 cups flour and yeast. Heat milk, sugar, shortening, and salt to lukewarm. When heated, add to dry ingredients. Beat in eggs at low speed. By hand add 6 to 7 cups flour. Knead 8 to 10 minutes. Place in greased bowl. Cover; let rise until doubled (about 1 hour). Punch down. Divide into fourths for rolls and sixths for tea-rings.

Kristie, Jessica, Jackie, Nate, & Katie enjoy sticky buns at Grandma Janette's.

THREE-HOUR BUNS

Great-great Grandma Ruggles

■ ■ ■ ■ ■ ■ ■ ■ ■ ■ ■

INGREDIENTS

4 cups warm milk

8 tablespoons sugar

3 tablespoons yeast

8 tablespoons shortening

2 teaspoons salt

6 cups flour

PREPARATION

Dissolve sugar and yeast in milk for 10 to 15 minutes. Add shortening, salt, and 2 cups flour. Beat until smooth. Add enough flour (about 4 cups) to make firm dough. Let rise 1 hour. Make into buns; let rise. Bake at 350°F for 50 to 60 minutes.

Courtney & Katie snack on "kid" buns at Grandma Janette's.

TRADITIONAL SWEET ROLL DOUGH
Debbie Oke

INGREDIENTS

2 packages yeast

1/2 cup warm water

1 1/2 cups lukewarm milk

1/2 cup sugar

2 teaspoons salt

2 eggs

1/2 cup butter or margarine

7 to 7 1/2 cups flour

PREPARATION

Dissolve yeast in warm water. Stir in milk, sugar, salt, eggs, butter or margarine, and 2 1/2 cups flour. Beat until smooth. Add enough flour to make dough easy to handle. Knead until smooth and elastic, about 5 minutes. Place in greased bowl, turn over. Cover. May be stored in refrigerator for 3 to 4 days. Let rise in warm place until doubled, about 1 1/2 hours. Punch down. Shape into rolls. Cover. Let rise until doubled (about 30 minutes). Bake at 375°F for 12 minutes.

Every man should eat and drink, and enjoy the good of all his labour, it is the gift of God.
Ecclesiastes 3:13

OATMEAL BREAD

Debbie Oke

■ ■ ■ ■ ■ ■ ■ ■ ■ ■ ■ ■

INGREDIENTS

2 packages yeast

1 cup warm water

2 cups oatmeal (uncooked)

2 1/2 cups boiling water

3/4 cup cooking oil

1 cup honey (or part corn syrup)

4 eggs (beaten)

1 to 2 tablespoons salt

2 cups whole wheat flour

1 cup wheat bran (may use flour)

6 to 7 cups white flour

PREPARATION

Dissolve yeast in warm water. In small bowl, pour boiling water over oatmeal. Set aside to cool until lukewarm. Beat all ingredients (except white flour) together, making sure everything is lukewarm. Work in white flour to make a nice dough. Knead 8 to 10 minutes. Place in greased bowl. Let double twice. Shape into loaves or rolls. Let rise. Bake at 400°F for 10 minutes, then reduce heat to 350°F and bake 25 to 30 minutes for loaves, or 15 to 20 minutes for rolls.

26
...
Zest & Zip

GENERAL HINTS FOR FLAVORING

■ ■ ■ ■ ■ ■ ■ ■ ■ ■ ■ ■

1. Store herbs in driest, coolest, darkest place in the kitchen. Be sure to date the containers so you will know how long you have had them.

2. Fresh garlic usually loses its full strength after 6 months. Always store it in a container with a loose-fitting lid.

3. Herbs that can be stored up to 1 year without losing potency or flavor: basil, bay, caraway, chives, coriander, dill, fennel, marjoram, mint, oregano, parsley, savory, shallots, and tarragon.

4. Herbs that can be stored up to 2 years: nutmeg (whole), peppercorns, rosemary, sage, and thyme.

5. Use a small amount of one or more herbs to enhance the flavor of food. You should not be able to recognize a definite herb flavor. Try $1/2$ teaspoon per pint for liquid food or for 1 pound of fish or chicken.

6. Each herb has a characteristic oil that gives its flavor or fragrance to food. Chop very fine if using fresh herbs so more of the oils can escape.

7. Heat releases the oil of the herbs quickly. Cold does not.

8. In cold juices, cheese, etc., herbs should be presoaked or added several hours before serving. In hot soups or stews, herbs are added